C0-AOH-065

Cambridge Texts and Studies in Education

TEXTS

FÉNELON ON EDUCATION

FÉNELON ON EDUCATION

A TRANSLATION OF THE 'TRAITÉ DE L'ÉDUCATION DES FILLES' AND OTHER DOCUMENTS ILLUSTRATING FÉNELON'S EDUCATIONAL THEORIES AND PRACTICE, TOGETHER WITH AN INTRODUCTION AND NOTES

BY

H. C. BARNARD

Emeritus Professor of Education in the University of Reading

CAMBRIDGE
AT THE UNIVERSITY PRESS
1966

PUBLISHED BY
THE SYNDICS OF THE CAMBRIDGE UNIVERSITY PRESS

Bentley House, 200 Euston Road, London N.W. 1
American Branch: 32 East 57th Street, New York, N.Y. 10022
West African Office: P.M.B. 5181, Ibadan, Nigeria

Printed in Great Britain at the University Printing House, Cambridge
(*Brooke Crutchley, University Printer*)

LIBRARY OF CONGRESS CATALOGUE
CARD NUMBER: 66-10450

CONTENTS

INTRODUCTION *page* vii

I Life of Fénelon vii

II Fénelon as an educationist xxx

III Some bibliographical notes xliii

THE EDUCATION OF GIRLS 1

ADVICE TO A LADY OF QUALITY CONCERNING THE EDUCATION OF HER DAUGHTER 97

ANTIOPE—FÉNELON'S IDEAL OF WOMANHOOD (FROM TÉLÉMAQUE) 108

MEMORANDUM ON THE EDUCATION OF THE DUC DE BOURGOGNE AND HIS BROTHERS 111

PROGRAMMES OF STUDIES FOR THE DUC DE BOURGOGNE FOR THE YEARS 1695 AND 1696 (LETTERS TO THE ABBÉ FLEURY) 117

EXAMINATION OF CONSCIENCE ON THE DUTIES OF ROYALTY 122

POPULAR EDUCATION (FROM TÉLÉMAQUE) 132

NOTES 134

CHRONOLOGICAL TABLE 145

INDEX 148

ACKNOWLEDGEMENTS

I would like to acknowledge with gratitude the help which I have received from Professor A. C. F. Beales, of King's College, London, and from the staff of the Reading University Library.

H. C. B.

INTRODUCTION

I. *Life of Fénelon*

FRANÇOIS DE SALIGNAC* DE LA MOTHE-FÉNELON was born on 6 August 1651, at the castle of Fénelon in Périgord. This château, situated in one of the most delightful parts of France, still exists. It was the home of an ancient and distinguished family, but Fénelon's father, Pons de Salignac, Comte de la Mothe-Fénelon, was one of the *noblesse de province* who had remained on their estates and, unlike the *noblesse de cour*, had not emigrated to Versailles, there to bask in the radiance of *Le Roi Soleil* and to benefit from the promotions and pensions that this often implied. Owing to the decline in the value of feudal dues and of the purchasing power of money, many families of the old provincial nobility had become impoverished; and this was, to some extent at any rate, the case with the Fénelons. As Saint-Simon has said, 'Fénelon was a nobleman without wealth'.† Pons de Salignac had been twice married. By his first wife he had eleven children and by the second four more. François de Salignac, the Fénelon with whom we are concerned, was a child of the second marriage. Of his childhood and early education little is known. He had delicate health and was therefore brought up at home. Here he was entrusted to a tutor who succeeded in giving him 'a more extensive acquaintance with the Greek and Latin languages than is normally achieved at so early an age'.‡ This aptitude and love for the classics

* An alternative spelling is *Salagnac*.

† *Mémoires* (ed. Chéruel, 1856–8), I, 176.

‡ Cardinal de Bausset, *Histoire de Fénelon* (1808, 1850), I, 9.

remained characteristic of Fénelon throughout his life. Under the *Ancien Régime* a career in the Church was the normal destiny of a younger son of a noble family, whether he had any vocation for such work or not. But in Fénelon's case there seems to have been a real bent in that direction; and this strengthened as he grew older and qualified him particularly as a 'spiritual director'. More worldly considerations included the fact that one of his uncles was bishop of the neighbouring see of Sarlat, and another, Antoine, Marquis de Fénelon, whose fortune was much superior to that of Fénelon's father, was closely associated with Jean-Jacques Olier, the founder of the famous Parisian seminary of Saint-Sulpice. Thus the young Fénelon would not lack benefactors in the ecclesiastical career which lay before him. In 1663, then, at the age of twelve he entered the University of Cahors where in the Faculty of Arts he took the course in humanities and philosophy which would correspond roughly to that of the upper forms of a modern British grammar school and was not what we should nowadays regard as university work. Thence he migrated to the University of Paris and became a member of the Collège du Plessis. But in 1668 his uncle, Antoine de Fénelon, transferred him to the seminary of Saint-Sulpice and there put him under the tutorship of Louis Tronson. In founding Saint-Sulpice, Olier had aimed at contributing to the revival of priestly life in France which had indirectly been stimulated by the Council of Trent and which was one of the features of the Counter-Reformation.* The Oratorians, founded by Cardinal de Bérulle, and the Lazarists or Prêtres de la Mission of St Vincent de Paul were devoted to the same end.

* See H. L. Sidney Lear, *The Revival of Priestly Life in Seventeenth Century France* (1877).

The influence of Saint-Sulpice and of Tronson upon Fénelon was deep and lasting. In a letter which he wrote to Le Tellier, the confessor of Louis XIV, he says of the seminary that 'nothing more venerable and apostolic can be found',* and he commends it to the good offices of the king. And of his tutor, Tronson, he says in a letter to Pope Clement XI: 'I congratulate myself on having had M. Tronson for my instructor in the Word of Life and having been formed under his personal care for the ecclesiastical state. Never was any man superior to him in love of discipline, in skill, prudence, piety and insight into character.'† It was while he was at Saint-Sulpice that Fénelon was ordained priest—in the year 1674 or 1675; and probably through the influence of his uncle, the Bishop of Sarlat, he was chosen as representative of the diocese of Bordeaux at the Assembly of Clergy in 1675. At Saint-Sulpice he exercised his ministry in the parish, and in particular was entrusted with the duty of expounding the Scriptures on Sundays and holy-days. But he had other aspirations. One of his elder half-brothers, who had preceded him at Saint-Sulpice, had already departed as a missionary to Canada; and Fénelon himself, combining the enthusiasms of an evangelist and a classical scholar, formed the project of joining a mission to the Levant. In a letter dated 9 October 1675‡ he says: 'All Greece opens before me. The Sultan retires in terror. The Peloponnese draws the breath of liberty. The Church of Corinth blossoms again. The voice of the Apostle is heard there once more. I feel myself transported to those beautiful places and among those precious ruins to recapture the very spirit of antiquity....

* *Œuvres* (1858), v, 771.

† See W. H. Jervis, *History of the Church of France* (1872), II, 5.

‡ *Œuvres*, v, 214.

O blessed Patmos, I shall kiss the ground where the Apostle trod and see the heavens opened....I shall see schism overthrown and East and West united, and the land sanctified by the steps of our Saviour and soaked with His blood delivered from the infidels and clothed with a new glory'...and much more to the same effect. But though this project illustrates Fénelon's chief interests at this period, it was destined not to be fulfilled. In deference to the wishes of his family, and perhaps also of Tronson, he continued to serve in the parish of Saint-Sulpice. His work, however, attracted the attention of François de Harlai, the Archbishop of Paris; and he had also become very friendly with Bossuet. It is hardly surprising therefore that in 1678 he should have received the important appointment of superior of the *Nouvelles Catholiques* of Paris. This was a community of girls converted to Catholicism. Fénelon left Saint-Sulpice and went to live with his uncle the Marquis, to whom the king had granted apartments in the Abbey of Saint-Germain-des-Prés.

It is perhaps difficult for a man of the twentieth century to understand—or, at any rate, to sympathise with—the motives which led Fénelon to accept this post; but it is necessary to realise the background against which it was set. The wars of religion which had distracted France during the second half of the sixteenth century were a struggle between a Catholic majority and a not inconsiderable Huguenot minority. They were marked by atrocities on both sides. The St Bartholomew massacre of 1572 is the outstanding example; but the Huguenots were also capable of barbarities which—as in the case of their co-religionists in England—are not always so widely publicised. But with the accession of Henri IV and the promulgation of the Edict of Nantes (1598)

Protestants in France were allowed a measure of toleration such as was enjoyed by few—if any—religious minorities in other countries at this period. The Huguenots were granted freedom of conscience and full civil rights. They were permitted to exercise public worship almost everywhere and to open schools wherever they had churches. No student was to be debarred from any university, college or school on the grounds of belonging to the reformed religion, and Huguenot fathers, either during their lifetime or by will after death, might arrange for the education of their children exactly as they wished.

As a guarantee the Protestants were allowed to garrison and retain complete control of 142 *places de sûreté*, mainly in the west, centre and south of France. Of these La Rochelle, Montauban and Montpellier were the most important. This era of toleration, however, did not last long. The cry was raised that the Huguenots wished to set up a republic within the State itself, on the lines of the United Provinces of Holland. By the 1620's strife had already broken out again; and although the Peace of Montpellier reaffirmed to Huguenots the freedom of worship and civil equality which had been granted by the Edict of Nantes, in effect it curtailed the privileges allowed to them. They were no longer permitted to hold fortified cities or to convene general assemblies for political purposes. During the régime of Richelieu and under the increasingly despotic rule of Louis XIV the persecution of the Huguenots was intensified. In his *Mémoires* the king explicitly records his policy towards his Protestant subjects. 'I thought', he says, 'that the best way of gradually stamping them out was, firstly, not to subject them to any rigours and to continue what they had obtained from my predecessors, but to make no concessions beyond that, and to restrict the exercise of these within the narrowest limits which justice and decency allows.'* Even this ungenerous policy was changed into something more active with Louis's growing belief that the mere existence of a schismatic body within his dominions was a menace to absolutism; and under the influence of the king's confessor, Père la Chaise, and Mme de Maintenon, whom he privately married in 1684, and with the general support of the Church of France, severe measures were taken to stamp out the reformed religion. At first an attempt was made to convert Protestants by offering rewards and privileges to 'New Catholics', and excluding recalcitrants from offices and professions. More savage methods were exerted by bands of dragoons who terrorised large numbers of Protestants into at any rate a verbal abjuration of their faith. The Revocation of the Edict of Nantes in 1685 completed the work of persecution. Protestant worship was proscribed and Protestant churches and schools were demolished. Children of Huguenot parents were torn from their homes and sent to Catholic schools; thousands of Protestants escaped from France carrying their skills and experience to other countries; many more who remained were imprisoned or sent to the galleys; and many, too, who were forcibly converted remained rebellious at heart. Yet there is no doubt that the policy of Louis XIV with regard to the Huguenots was endorsed by the majority of French people. Some of the most estimable Catholics of the time—for example, Bossuet, La Bruyère, La Fontaine, Mme de Maintenon, Mme de Sévigné—fully approved of the revocation of the Edict of Nantes, though they may have deplored the manner in which the decree was executed.

* *Mémoires*, II, 456.

It is in this last group that Fénelon must be included, and it is therefore not a matter of surprise that he should have accepted a post involving the conversion of 'heretics'. The persecution of the reformed religion under Louis XIV had even more a political than a religious aim. But Fénelon put the religious aspect first. After all, he was a Catholic priest. For him the faith as interpreted by the Church was final and binding, and resistance to its doctrines was wicked because it was a menace to the truth and an insult to God himself. And since, from Fénelon's point of view, Church and State were intimately allied, the employment of the secular arm for the conversion of 'heretics' could be regarded as not merely permissible but even laudable. The *Nouvelles Catholiques* was a sisterhood which had been established as far back as 1634 and was under the direct protection of the king. It was 'designed to furnish young Protestant female converts with safe retreats against the persecution of their parents and the wiles of the heretics'.* There is no doubt that in some cases the girls and young women had been taken from their homes against their wish and without their parents' consent. They were committed to the charge of a Mother Superior and ordered to make submission within a specified time. If they remained obdurate they might be removed to a prison or even banished. But in many cases they seem to have been orphans from Protestant families, or girls whose families contained members of both the Catholic and Reformed churches. Mme de Maintenon was herself an example of this, though her conversion was effected not through the *Nouvelles Catholiques*, but through a convent of the ordinary kind.

* Quoted from *Constitutions pour la Maison des Nouvelles Catholiques* (1675).

The actual administration of a community of 'New Catholics' was in the hands of the Mother Superior who acted under the direction of the government; but Fénelon's duties at the Paris convent were rather those of a visitor or spiritual adviser. His part was to teach, explain, persuade and guide. We can get some idea of his methods from his *Traité du Ministère des Pasteurs* and a long sermon preached on the occasion of the taking of the veil by a 'nouvelle convertie'. In the former Fénelon advances the usual arguments about the enormous variety of interpretation of the Scriptures which results from leaving them to individual judgment rather than to the inspired decision of the Catholic Church. He stresses the apostolic succession which is possessed by Catholic priests, but not by Protestant pastors. As for these latter, 'Even when they speak the truth their words are only the words of a man and not of God. Their ordination has no value. Their communion is no real communion nor the sacrament of the Saviour. In short, their church is no church at all.'* In the sermon Fénelon returns to the uncertainty and unreliability of Scripture if left to the interpretation of the individual. This implies 'trampling underfoot the greatest authority which Providence has established under heaven, in order to set up a supreme tribunal in one's heart'.† He goes on to deal with those aspects of Catholic doctrine which had been rejected by Protestantism—the use of Latin in the liturgy, the real presence in the Eucharist, the life of the cloister, prayers for the dead. There is no note of blame, but rather the gracious compassion of one who is seeking to bring back a wayward child to the right path. How far Fénelon approved of forcible measures and the cruelties by which many of the *Nouvelles Catholiques*

* *Œuvres*, I, 357–8. † *Œuvres*, III, 346.

had been recruited may perhaps be doubted; but it is a question which becomes more insistent in reference to a missionary campaign to which he was appointed in 1685.

This was part of the intensified drive against the Huguenots which led up to and followed the revocation of the Edict of Nantes in the same year. As has already been indicated, the government's method of attempting to stamp out Protestantism was to send soldiery to Huguenot districts where they were billeted on the inhabitants and encouraged to force them by cruelty and licence into abjuration of their faith. When these *dragonnades* had ostensibly accomplished their purpose, the soldiers were withdrawn and replaced by missionaries from Paris. As Mme de Sévigné says in a letter dated 28 October 1685, 'So far the dragoons have been excellent missionaries; the clergy who are now being sent will complete the work.'* The area assigned to Fénelon and his colleagues was that of Aunis and Saintonge, near the mouth of the Garonne and in the neighbourhood of La Rochelle which was the chief citadel of French Protestantism. The mission arrived in December 1685, two months after the revocation of the Edict, and it lasted until July 1686. It was renewed from May to July of the following year. Several letters written by Fénelon during this period give us some idea of his methods, his hopes, and the difficulties with which he had to contend. 'A short visit', he says, 'which we have just paid to Marennes worked marvels. It succeeded in winning over the most difficult cases. Since this time we have found people more keen and amenable. They still have religious difficulties, but otherwise almost all

* *Lettres de Mme de Sévigné*, ed. A. Regnier (1925), VII, 470.

of them admit that we have shown them, with abundant evidence, that, according to Scripture, they must submit to the Church, and that there is no objection to Catholic doctrine which we have not completely met.... Provided that this good beginning is continued by friendly preachers, who combine a talent for instruction with an ability to inspire confidence, these people will soon be true Catholics.'* But there were none the less misgivings and the task was not always easy. In March 1686 in a letter to Bossuet Fénelon says: 'The half-converted Huguenots are attached to their religion with a horrible excess of obstinacy; but as soon as the rigour of their penalties is made plain their strength abandons them. Whereas the martyrs were humble, docile, fearless and incapable of dissimulation, these are cowardly in the face of force, stubborn against the truth, and up to all sorts of hypocrisy.... They are a most dangerous leaven in a nation. By their perjury they have so profaned the most holy things that there are few signs left by which one can recognise those whose conversion is sincere. One can only pray to God for them and not be disheartened by having to instruct them.'† Fénelon showed little sympathy or toleration for those who clung to their religion; but if one is a missionary one has at least to be utterly convinced of the truth of one's own particular gospel and the iniquitous falsehood of the religion which one has to combat. Fénelon also realised the political dangers of possible contacts between the Huguenots of France and the Protestants of Holland. But except in the case of incorrigible 'heretics' he seems to have relied on gentle methods. He secured a supply of corn for the starving population with whom he had to deal. He ensured to poverty-stricken converts the continued payment of a

* *Œuvres*, v, 221. † *Œuvres*, v, 227.

dole which they had been receiving from the local Huguenot consistory. He preferred conversion through the medium of schools and teachers and the distribution of Catholic literature to the drastic methods of force and persecution. But it is clear from his letters that he relinquished his missionary endeavours without regret. In March 1686 he writes: 'Our converts are going on a little better, but progress is extremely slow. It is no small matter to change the convictions of an entire people.'* And again in July 1687: 'I continue to believe that we ought to leave the people in peace. It is obvious that the harvest is not yet ripe and we must not try to ripen it in a hurry.'† So Fénelon returned to Paris and resumed his work with the *Nouvelles Catholiques*. The Saintonge mission is not a very pleasant episode in his career. Like most Catholic Frenchmen of his day he did not realise the implications of the persecution of the Huguenots and the revocation of the Edict of Nantes, and of the resulting disasters to France which were soon to become obvious. It may be, also, that he eventually realised the folly of attempting wholesale conversions by the use of force, or even of persuasion. In his *Examen de Conscience sur les Devoirs de la Royauté*, which he drew up about 1711 for the instruction of the Duke of Burgundy he says quite definitely, 'Above all never force your subjects to change their religion. No human power can penetrate the last defences of the human heart. Men can never be convinced by force; it only creates hypocrites. When kings meddle with religion, instead of protecting it, they enslave it. Allow political freedom to all, not approving everything as though you were indifferent, but suffering with patience whatever God

* *Œuvres*, v, 227.

† *Lettres Inédites*, ed. Verlaque (1874), p. 59.

allows and endeavouring to win men by gentle persuasion.'*

It has already been said that while Fénelon was still acting as superior of the *Nouvelles Catholiques* he had gone to live with his uncle, the Marquis Antoine de Fénelon. Among the latter's intimate friends was the Duc de Beauvillier† and his brother-in-law, the Duc de Chevreuse. Both of them had married daughters of the financier Colbert; and they and their wives were members of the sober-minded coterie at the Court, gathered around Mme de Maintenon and not without influence on Louis himself in his reformed old age. De Beauvillier in 1685 had been appointed Chef du Conseil des Finances, which was 'essentially the Council of Administration of the Monarchy';‡ but Saint-Simon comments how unworldly he was, indifferent to intrigues and preferment—more like a monk than a statesman. He and his wife had a family of nine daughters, and it was at the Duchess's request that, soon after his appointment to the *Nouvelles Catholiques*, Fénelon wrote his *Traité de l'Éducation des Filles*, a translation of which is given on pp. 1–96. The book was not published till 1687, but it scored an immediate success and has remained one of the most important and popular of Fénelon's literary productions. But it was also one of the factors which led to his appointment in 1689 as *précepteur* to the Dauphin's eldest son, the Duc de Bourgogne. It was customary for a prince of the royal house in contemporary France to be en-

* *Œuvres*, v, 39.

† This name is often spelt Beauvilliers, but the *Bibliographie Universelle* (1811–28) says that it is wrong to add the final 's'. I have therefore adopted the form 'Beauvillier'. This is the spelling given in the *Dictionnaire de Biographie Française* (1951) and in the *Grand Larousse* (1960).

‡ See *Modern France*, ed. Tilley (1922), p. 62.

trusted to a 'governess' for the first seven years of his life. He was then put under the care of a *gouverneur* who was given complete responsibility for his pupil and had to be in constant attendance upon him. The governor was always a courtier or soldier of distinction, and in the case of the Duc de Bourgogne it was the Duc de Beauvillier who had been appointed to this office in August 1689. At the same time the young prince was given a suite which included a *précepteur* or tutor who was associated with the governor and was more particularly responsible for the intellectual and moral and religious education of their charge. In the case of the Dauphin himself the *précepteur* had been no less a person than Bossuet, the foremost churchman of his day.* It is not surprising therefore that the first act of the Duc de Beauvillier on his appointment was to invite Fénelon to co-operate with him by acting as *précepteur* to the young Duke.† The Abbé Fleury, who had been a colleague of Fénelon's in the Saintonge mission, became his assistant or *sous-gouverneur*. He had already produced his *Traité du Choix et de la Méthode d'Études* which was published in 1686 and which is one of the most interesting and valuable educational treatises of the period. In 1690 the Duc de Bourgogne's younger brother, the Duc d'Anjou (who eventually became Philip V, King of Spain) also came under the care of the *gouverneur* and the *précepteur*. Three years later the Dauphin's youngest son, the Duc de Berry, joined the group.

The appointment of De Beauvillier and Fénelon was very generally approved. The education of a prince who

* See H. C. Barnard, *The French Tradition in Education* (1922), ch. IV.

† The *Bibliographie Universelle* (XXXIX, p. 51) says that it was the *Traité de l'Éducation des Filles* 'which revealed to the Duc de Beauvillier the extent of the author's genius'.

was Louis XIV's grandson and might one day become King of France was regarded as a matter of the highest national importance. Under the régime of the enlightened despot the task of enlightening him and preparing him for the duties or his office was obviously one of the greatest responsibility; and the fact that the Duc de Bourgogne's early death prevented him from fulfilling his expected destiny did not at the time lessen the significance of the work of De Beauvillier and Fénelon. But their task proved to be no easy one. The Duc de Bourgogne seems to have been a mass of contradictions. Saint-Simon gives a dark picture of his character in his early years, but there seems some reason for believing that the portrait is overdrawn.* Fénelon himself provides what is perhaps a more reliable account of his pupil's disposition: 'When he lacks an excuse for attacking others he turns against himself. He blames himself and says he is good for nothing, he grows discouraged and takes it ill if anyone tries to console him. He wants to be alone and yet can't endure solitude.... Sometimes he can't prevent himself from being astonished at his own excuses and outbursts of passion. In spite of his annoyance he will smile at the unbridled things that he has said.... In his most extraordinary and unreasonable fits of temper he can be agreeable, glib, clever, full of new turns, though he remains completely unreasonable.... When he is angry he doesn't mind what happens; he doesn't love anybody, nobody loves him, he is being persecuted or deceived, he doesn't want to have anything to do with anyone. But wait a moment, and behold quite a different scene. He wants to be on good terms with everybody—he loves them and they love him. He flatters and ingratiates himself, he bewitches even

* See J. Lemaître, *Fénelon* (1910), pp. 101–5.

those who were utterly unable to put up with him. He acknowledges his faults and laughs at his own excuses.'* Such then was the child of seven for whose upbringing De Beauvillier and Fénelon were made responsible. Their régime, which is described below,† had a profound effect upon him. 'The wonder is', says Saint-Simon, 'that in a very short time devotion and grace made a different man of him and changed so many serious faults into quite opposite virtues. Out of this abyss we saw emerge a prince who was pleasant, humane, generous, patient, modest, humble and abstemious. His only ambition was to unite the duties of a son and of a subject to those for which he thought he was destined.'‡

Although Fénelon's tutorship came to an end when the Duc de Bourgogne was only thirteen years old, he continued to supervise his education from a distance and to compose literary works directly designed to give him moral instruction which would fit him for the kingly duties to which he would one day succeed.§ Throughout the Duke's subsequent career Fénelon endeavoured to carry on a correspondence with his old pupil, and he never hesitated to give him the soundest advice even if that implied a criticism of his grandfather's administration. When in 1711 the death of the Dauphin made the Duc de Bourgogne direct heir to the throne, the exchange of letters became even more frequent. In 1697 he had married the charming Marie-Adelaide de Savoie,|| whose gaiety and good nature did something to enlighten the gloom of the latter years of Louis XIV. Soon afterwards

* *Œuvres*, III, 811–12. This *opusculum* has for its title 'le Fantasque'.

† See below, pp. 111–21. ‡ *Mémoires*, v, 196.

§ Especially *Télémaque*, *Fables*, and *Dialogues des Morts*. See below, pp. xxxvi–xl.

|| See below, p. 141.

he was put in command of the French army in Flanders, but his exploits in the War of the Spanish Succession were not such as to bring him much military glory. Public opinion blamed him for his share in the disastrous campaign of 1708. Finally, in 1712, both the Duc and the Duchesse de Bourgogne were carried off within a few days of each other by an infectious disease, leaving an infant son, Louis, as heir to the throne of France. So Fénelon's life-work of educating the prince who was to become an enlightened despot, concerned primarily with the good of his people, setting an example of personal and public morality, promoting the cause of peace and international goodwill, was destined to come to naught.

We must now turn back to Fénelon's own career from the year 1695 when he ceased officially to be tutor to the Duc de Bourgogne. In February of that year he was nominated to the archbishopric of Cambrai, and on 10 July he was consecrated in the chapel of Saint-Cyr, the school for the daughters of impoverished nobles which had been founded by Mme de Maintenon in 1686, and which in many ways was being run on lines similar to those which Fénelon had laid down in his *Traité de l'Éducation des Filles*. As has been said, however, he did not altogether lose touch with his work as tutor and adviser to the Duc de Bourgogne. In a letter* to the Marquise de Laval, dated 4 February 1695, and sent from Versailles, he says: 'I shall continue as *précepteur* to the princes by sharing my residence in my diocese (which is only thirty-five leagues from here) with my educational duties.' In another letter, written a few days later, he says: 'I shall reside for nine months of the year at Cambrai and give three months to my duties as preceptor'. But difficulties were destined to arise which

* *Œuvres*, V, 273.

affected the whole course of Fénelon's future career. In the year 1688 he had made the acquaintance of a certain Mme Guyon who became famous as the exponent of a set of doctrines known as Quietism. This was a form of mysticism which laid stress on contemplation and the cultivation of the inner spiritual life, to the neglect of 'works'. The Archbishop of Paris, realising the danger of such doctrines, had Mme Guyon confined to a convent, but her friends, who included Mme de Maintenon, secured her release, and for a time she exercised some influence among the nuns and girls at Saint-Cyr. Fénelon was also attracted by her teaching and gave expression to it in his *Explication des Maximes des Saints sur la Vie Intérieure*, published in January 1697. The book was promptly attacked by Bossuet and a bitter controversy ensued. Fénelon appealed to Rome, and finally in March 1699 twenty-three propositions extracted from the work were formally condemned in a papal brief. Fénelon, who had always preached submission to the decisions of the Church, promptly announced the condemnation from the pulpit of his cathedral at Cambrai and issued a pastoral letter in which he said: 'We confirm this brief, beloved brethren, both as regards the text of the book and the twenty-three propositions, simply, absolutely and without a shadow of reservation. We condemn both the book and the twenty-three propositions, in exactly their same form and with the same qualifications, simply, absolutely, and without reservation.' Fénelon also sent a letter of submission to the Pope.* However, one result of the Mme Guyon episode was that in August 1697 he had been banished from the Court and confined to his diocese. Louis XIV whole-

* See P. Janet, *Fénelon* (1892), p. 99, and *Œuvres*, letters 110–15 (pp. 409–21).

heartedly supported Bossuet in the controversy. Mme Guyon was imprisoned in the Bastille and not released until 1703. Meanwhile Fénelon's annual three-months' visits to supervise the Duc de Bourgogne's education came to an end, although as far as possible by his correspondence and other writings he continued to instruct and advise him.

For the last fifteen years of his life Fénelon remained in his diocese where he showed himself to be a true Father in God. His charity, the punctiliousness with which he performed his duties, his regular visitations which brought him into contact with every corner of his diocese, his graciousness and gentleness, won all hearts. 'As for his clergy, he left everyone at peace in his place, and instructed the priests he had brought with him to do their utmost to consider the feelings of the Flemings. On one occasion he severely reprimanded them for having wished to compel children to recite the catechism in French. He retained on his staff the colleagues of his predecessor and took care to choose his vicars-general from among the clergy of his diocese. He never decided any matter without consulting the members of the chapter of Cambrai. Thus he soon succeeded in dissipating any prejudices which the Flemings might have against an archbishop who had been born in Périgord and who arrived straight from Versailles. One soon forgot that he was not a native of Flanders when one saw how little inclined he was to despise the inhabitants of this country, and how determined he was to do them justice.'*

Fénelon retained the dignity which was natural to a scion of a noble family who was familiar with the life of the Court at Versailles; but he was always modest, kind

* E. de Broglie, *Fénelon à Cambrai* (1884), p. 209.

and hospitable. We have a picture of him in his palace at Cambrai, drawn by Bossuet's secretary, the Abbé Le Dieu, who was on a visit to him. 'The archbishop was wearing a long violet robe, cassock and chimere, with scarlet buttons and button-holes. He had no girdle or gold tassels, but he wore a plain biretta of green silk and white gloves, but no cloak. As dinner had already been announced he got up and invited me to take my place at his table. All the guests were waiting in the dining-room. We washed our hands without any ceremony. The prelate said grace and sat down at the head of the table. The Abbé de Chanterac* was on his left, and everyone else took their places without distinction. The seat on his right was vacant and he signed to me to take it. The meal was served on a splendid scale—many soups, some good beef and mutton, all sorts of entrées and ragoûts, partridges and game, magnificent fruit, a good red wine but no beer, with spotless table-linen, good bread, and silver plates and cutlery. The archbishop made a point of helping me to all the delicacies, and I thanked him with my hat in my hand; and every time he never failed to raise his hat too.† The conversation was informal, pleasant—even amusing. The prelate took his turn to speak and left everybody a fair chance to do so. He himself ate very little and only light food. He drank

* For details about the Abbé de Chanterac see Bausset, *Histoire de Fénelon*, II, 430–1. He is described as 'a faithful friend of Fénelon, involved in his administrative cares, his confidant in all personal matters, and habitual witness of his works of charity and his labours'.

† The custom of wearing hats by men at meals is illustrated in many contemporary pictures (e.g. *Le Repas de Famille* by Mathieu Le Nain). Cf. also Morvan de Bellegarde, *Traité de Civilité* (1698), ch. XI, 101; and Saint-Simon (*Mémoires*, VIII, 182): 'A ces repas tout le monde étoit couvert; c'eût été un manque de respect de n'avoir pas son chapeau sur sa tête.'

nothing but two or three sips of a thin white wine. He is indeed extremely thin, but he looks in good health. I think it must be grief that wears him for he looks very troubled.'* But when the progress of the War of the Spanish Succession brought the horrors of the campaign surging through Flanders and into the very neighbourhood of Cambrai Fénelon devoted himself to the service of the sick and wounded and turned his episcopal palace and seminary into a hospital, supplying the inmates with drugs and delicacies. His court and gardens became a refuge for the peasants and their flocks, who had been driven from their homes by the advance of the Allies; and all of them were maintained by the archbishop at his own expense. Nor were his acts of mercy confined to the soldiers and civilians of his own country. He was no less concerned for the prisoners of war confined in his diocese. The result was that the enemy were reported to have protected his property, and that of those for whom he interceded, even more than the French troops themselves. As Saint-Simon says, 'Much as he was loved and revered throughout the King's dominions, his fame stood even higher wherever the King's enemies were the masters.'†

During his exile at Cambrai Fénelon had devoted much of his leisure time to literary work, although several of his books were not actually published until after his death. He was concerned mainly with theological or political subjects. In the former category comes his treatise on *The Authority of the Sovereign Pontiff* (1710), in which he provides a justification for his submission to the condemnation of his *Maxims of the Saints*. He also published in 1712 a *Treatise on the*

* François Le Dieu, *Journal*, ed. Guettée (1856), III, 142.

† *Mémoires*, VII, 275.

Existence and Attributes of God. His *Examination of Conscience on the Duties of Royalty** was composed for the benefit of the Duc de Bourgogne just after the death of the Dauphin in 1711 which had left him heir to the title and next in succession to the throne of France. Of special interest also are Fénelon's *Plans de Gouvernement*, worked out in collaboration with the Duc de Chevreuse and usually known as the *Tables de Chaulnes* (1711). These recommend the formation of effective local assemblies to counteract the excessive centralisation of the existing régime. Taxation should be lightened and fairly distributed. The States General should be convened every three years. The nobility should retain their 'rank in the State, supporting the Throne while remaining independent of the King'; and this would obviously suppress the *noblesse de cour* and imply the residence of nobles on their estates. Church and State, though independent, should help and support each other, and the Gallican Liberties† should be respected. Venality of offices should be abolished and trade encouraged along the lines initiated by Colbert.

But the one subject above all others which occupied Fénelon's literary labours from about 1702 onwards was his polemic against Jansenism. This 'heresy' owed its origin to a Flemish theologian named Jansen who, in a treatise on St Augustine, published in 1640, had set forth theories concerning Grace and Predestination which were not unlike those advocated by Calvin. The book was fiercely attacked by the Jesuits and condemned by the Vatican; but the Jansenists made powerful friends in France and included in their ranks some of the most saintly souls of the period—for example, Pascal, Dr Arnauld, and many of the nuns and solitaries connected

* See below, pp. 122–31. † See *Camb. Mod. Hist.* v, 74.

with the convent of Port-Royal. The controversy raged on and off throughout the rest of the seventeenth century; but—as with the Protestantism of the Huguenots—it had its political, as well as its theological side, and Louis XIV, instigated by his Jesuit confessors La Chaise and Le Tellier, began a renewed attack on Jansenism. The papal bull *Unigenitus* in 1713 was designed as a final condemnation of the movement; but the controversy rumbled on well into the eighteenth century, and even today there are still some Jansenist survivals in France and Holland. One may be tempted to believe that Fénelon's championship of orthodoxy and his partisanship with the Jesuits in the opposition to Jansenism were in some degree an attempt to make amends for the *Maxims of the Saints* and the suspicion of heresy which had attached itself to his name and had resulted in the papal brief of 1699. But he never advocated the cruel persecution of the sect which led to such atrocities as the destruction of the monastery of Port-Royal des Champs and the desecration of its cemetery (1709–11). Fénelon's own diocese of Cambrai contained many Jansenists, and the University of Louvain, where Jansen himself had been a professor, still exercised much influence on theological attitudes in Flanders. But Fénelon's method of dealing with them was that which he had used in the case of the Protestants of Saintonge and Aunis. However much he might condemn the movement in his writings, his tolerance and friendly persuasiveness won him respect even among the Jansenists themselves. If we may believe Saint-Simon, 'The Low Countries were crowded with Jansenists or people reputed as such. Fénelon's diocese in particular and even Cambrai itself were full of them. But both alike were havens of rest and peace for them. Happy and contented in finding a refuge there they were not in the least put out by their archbishop who, although disagreeing with their doctrine, left them in peace. They left others to defend their tenets and did little to undermine the general affection which everybody felt for Fénelon.'* There seems some reason for thinking that this estimate is possibly exaggerated, but the fact remains that Fénelon relied less on persecution and punishment than on education and the reformation of seminaries and colleges in which the Jansenist doctrines were being propagated.

Fénelon's closing years were clouded with a succession of bereavements. The Duc de Chevreuse died in 1712 and the Duc de Beauvillier in 1714. As has been said, the death of the Dauphin in 1711 had left the Duc de Bourgogne heir to the throne; but the latter's death in 1712 shattered Fénelon's hopes and dealt him a blow from which he never recovered. He was involved in a carriage accident which, although he escaped injury, undermined his feeble condition. On New Year's Day 1715 he was attacked by a 'sharp fever of unknown origin', and after six days of pain and distress he died peacefully in the early morning of 7 January. His apostolic virtues as an archbishop were illustrated by the fact that he left practically nothing for his heirs. 'His revenues had been completely swallowed up by losses and great expenses caused by the presence of the armies during the last three campaigns, especially as he had never economised on the charities which he bestowed on the convents of this city, on the poor of his diocese, on the Sisters of Charity who look after the sick poor, on the parishes which he used to visit, on the students in his diocese and on a multitude of other persons.'†

* *Mémoires*, VI, 87.

† Bausset, *Histoire de Fénelon*, IV, 440–1.

Saint-Simon describes Fénelon as a tall, thin man, well built, with a large nose and eyes full of fire and expression—the sort of person whom, once seen, one never forgets. As can be gathered even from this short account of his career, his personality was a complex one. He came of an ancient and noble family and he never lost the dignity of a high-born prelate associated with the Court and the archiepiscopal palace. He suggested, says Saint-Simon, at once the man of letters, the bishop and the great noble. What struck one above all in his character was his shrewdness, his intelligence, his graciousness and good manners—above all, his nobility. Yet he was always acutely conscious of the needs of the poor and suffering, and of the responsibilities towards them of those in high places. As a spiritual director he exercised a deep and wide influence. His letters dealing with matters of conscience and conduct form a large and important part of his literary output. He belongs to the *Ancien Régime*, yet he is deeply critical of it, and, particularly in many of his political views, he looks forward to the philosophy of the eighteenth century. If Louis XIV had not lived so long and if the Duc de Bourgogne had survived to become king, with Fénelon as the power behind the throne, the principles laid down in the *Duties of Royalty* and the *Tables de Chaulnes* might have been put into practice, and the whole course of subsequent French history might have been profoundly affected.

II. *Fénelon as an educationist*

Fénelon's educational theories and practice centre round his *Traité de l'Éducation des Filles* and his work as tutor and adviser to the Dauphin's eldest son, the Duc de Bourgogne. It is to these two subjects in particular, therefore, that we must now give our attention. In the article on Fénelon in the *Encyclopædia Britannica* the treatise on the education of girls is said to be the 'first systematic attempt ever made to deal with that subject as a whole'. This is hardly true. As far back as the early days of Christianity St Jerome, in his letters to Laeta and Gaudentius, had done exactly what Fénelon achieved in his treatise; that is to say, he gave advice on the bringing-up of an individual girl, but in so doing outlined a whole scheme of female education. Such ideas lay dormant for many centuries, but even in the Middle Ages there was a movement—and a counter-movement—for giving women more freedom and greater educational opportunities. The subject is treated in considerable detail by Gustave Reynier in the first chapter of his *La Femme au XVIIe Siècle* (Paris, 1929) and in his *Les Femmes Savantes de Molière* (Paris, 1948), pp. 8–27. The Renaissance saw a renewed interest in female education and the rightful position of women in society. Vives and Erasmus wrote extensively on these subjects, and the former in particular gave detailed advice on the methods which should be employed in the education of girls. But all these writers had in mind the upbringing of the daughters of 'upper-class' families. It was left to the Protestant reformers, like Luther and Comenius, to advocate systems of popular education in which boys and girls, rich and poor, alike should share.

With regard to the actual state of the 'woman question' in France in the latter part of the seventeenth century one has to remember that it had excited a good deal of attention, and the development of the *salons* and *préciosité* illustrates this. The influence exerted by women in society and in politics was never stronger than at this period. As a papal nuncio had said, as far back as 1623, 'En France tous les grands évènements, toutes les intrigues d'importance, dépendent le plus souvent des femmes.'* The question at once suggests itself 'How were these women educated?' I have dealt with this subject at length in my *Girls at School under the Ancien Régime* (1954). It can be said shortly that as far as the poorer classes were concerned many girls received very little instruction. All the same, there were 'little schools', parish charity schools, and elementary schools run by various religious orders which did give some rudimentary teaching in reading and religion to girls as well as to boys. Girls of the bourgeoisie or the nobility were educated either in convents—which differed enormously in effectiveness, type of curriculum and the amenities offered—or else at home by 'governesses'. But teachers of this type were sometimes little better than ignorant servants and little fitted to give intellectual instruction. It was in society itself, and particularly through the art of conversation which one learnt there, that many of the outstanding women of the period had really received their main education. But there was also a demand for courses of popular lectures—sometimes even on scientific subjects—and these were much patronised by women of the 'upper classes'. For example, the poet and etymologist Ménage founded a *petite académie* which met every Wednesday and included among its pupils Mme de Sévigné, the Princesse de Guéménée and the young lady who subsequently became Mme de la Fayette. This was only one of several such institutions in which literary, philosophical and scientific instruction was made available to women as well as men.

Of course the movement for female education did not lack its critics, as we can see from Molière's *Femmes Savantes*, *École des Femmes*, and *Précieuses Ridicules*; but

* See Reynier, *La Femme au XVIIe Siècle* (1933), p. 28.

there was at the same time a strong feminist reaction. This is illustrated by the works of Poulain de la Barre, the first of which, *De l'Égalité des deux Sexes*, appeared in 1673. The author had studied at the Sorbonne and had been ordained. But subsequently he became a convert to Protestantism and retired to Geneva after the revocation of the Edict of Nantes. He claims that girls are by nature as capable of education as boys, and he sketches for them a curriculum including mathematics and science, history and philosophy. Girls need not be required to study the classics, but plenty of good French literature should be included in the syllabus. He advocates the training of 'governesses' who will be competent to deal with such a programme.

Just about the time that Fénelon was composing his *Traité de l'Éducation des Filles* there had occurred two events which undoubtedly influenced him. One was the foundation of Mme de Maintenon's school at Saint-Cyr, to which he became a frequent visitor. The other was the publication of Claude Fleury's *Du Choix et de la Méthode des Études*. Both of these events date from the year 1686. Fénelon made the acquaintance of Mme de Maintenon about 1688, through the intermediary of the Duc de Beauvillier. The Abbé Fleury had composed his treatise as early as 1675, though it was not published until eleven years later. It can hardly be just a coincidence that in the organisation and aims of Saint-Cyr Mme de Maintenon so often takes similar views to those of Fénelon; and that in Fleury's chapter on 'Études des Femmes' he seems to summarise Fénelon's recommendations on the education of girls. It is surely a justifiable inference that the three educationists were in touch with one another and familiar with each other's views. They agreed in regarding as unsatisfactory the type of contemporary education which was content to give a girl a purely formal religious education, together with a bare smattering of literacy and a training in social accomplishments and the usages of polite society. All three believed that women should not be regarded as an inferior sex even if their functions in society were not necessarily the same as those of man. Women, as Fénelon says, are 'half the human race, redeemed like the other half by the blood of Christ'. Fleury puts the same point equally strongly*—'as if their souls were of a different kind than those of men; as if they had not, like us, a reason to instruct, a will to govern, passions to subdue, health to preserve, property to administer, or as if it were easier for them than for us to fulfil all these duties without any knowledge'.

Mme de Maintenon, Fleury and Fénelon alike regard moral and intellectual education as inseparable. There is no need for girls to study the classics for we should not wish them to become blue-stockings. Even a knowledge of modern languages has its dangers because it may lead to a taste for novel-reading; but girls should learn to read and write their own language correctly. Arithmetic will be of value to the future housewife and girls should be trained to carry the responsibilities which will devolve on them when they have an estate to manage. Fénelon even recommends a tincture of legal information. But above all the girls should learn to exercise reason. Mme de Maintenon has a delightful picture of 'la fille raisonnable';† Fleury says: 'As for the mind, they must be trained from an early age to think consecutively and to

* Mlle de Gournay had put it more piquantly: 'Il n'est rien de plus semblable au chat sur une fenêtre, que la chatte.' ('There is nothing so like a male cat on a window-sill as a female cat.') (*Égalité des Hommes et des Femmes* (1622), p. 25.)

† *Lettres et Entretiens*, I, 342–4.

judge soundly on those everyday matters which may be useful to them.'* But a girl is not called upon to discuss theological problems. It is enough that she has learnt to think and to see things as they are, that she is well read but no *précieuse*, a good housewife and manager, sound in character and a faithful daughter of Mother Church.

Like Montaigne and Locke and Rousseau, Fénelon throughout his treatise is thinking of a pupil belonging to a family at any rate in easy circumstances and being brought up by a tutor or governess at home. He is not concerned with schools as such. It is true that in a passage in *Télémaque*, where he is describing the constitution of a utopia called Salente, he says that children belong to the State more than to their parents and that there should be a national system of education. But he seems to have borrowed this theory, like so much more of his account, from Plato's *Republic* or from an idealised reconstruction of the Spartan constitution. Although he was a churchman and had been director of the *Nouvelles Catholiques* he had considerable misgivings as to the value of conventual education. It all depends on the particular convent, but in order to avoid the risk it is better to bring up a girl in her own home. This implies, of course, that the mother—or the governess who takes her place—must be fitted for this task and ready to shoulder the responsibilities involved. It was in order to help her to do this that Fénelon composed his *Traité de l'Éducation des Filles*, primarily for the Duchesse de Beauvillier but ultimately for the benefit of any mother who was similarly placed. But in spite of its title the *Traité*, in its published form, is a good deal more than a treatise on the education of girls. Certain parts of the book do certainly refer specifically to the female sex; but roughly two-thirds

* *Traité du Choix*, pp. 291–2.

of it is equally applicable to the education of boys also. It is noticeable that in these chapters Fénelon uses the word 'enfants', and never 'filles'.

It was as *précepteur* to the Duc de Bourgogne, therefore, that Fénelon was able to put into practice many of the educational principles which he had laid down in the *Traité de l'Éducation des Filles*. But they are worked out in greater detail as regards method, and they are adapted to a boy, whose curriculum would be wider than that prescribed for daughters, and moreover for a boy who was, as it was supposed, destined one day to become king. Bossuet in a previous generation had acted as *précepteur* to the Dauphin who was the Duc de Bourgogne's father, and he has left us, in a letter to Pope Innocent XI, a fairly full account of the methods which he employed.* In the case of Fénelon we have no formal record of this type; but there is none the less a fair amount of indirect evidence. We have, for example, a memorandum on the education of the Duc de Bourgogne and his brothers which was drawn up by the Marquis de Louville. Some information about this is given on pp. xlvii–xlviii, and a translation of it will be found on pp. 111–16.

An indication of the intellectual content of the Duc de Bourgogne's education is also given in two letters which Fénelon wrote to the Abbé Fleury, who was the Duke's *sous-précepteur*. These deal with the curriculum for the years 1695 and 1696.† Here again intellectual instruction is regarded as a means to moral education. The task is not so much to inform the Duc de Bourgogne's mind as to reform his passionate and uncontrolled disposition. Thus Fénelon believes in putting his moral lessons in an attractive form and inculcating

* See H. C. Barnard, *The French Tradition in Education*, ch. IV.
† See below, pp. 117–21.

them indirectly; he also does his best to diversify instruction so that his pupil may not become bored. With this end in view Fénelon composed from time to time a series of fables, adapted to the developing capabilities of the young prince. They start with fairy tales and anecdotes about animals, and as the pupil grows older the subjects are drawn from classical antiquity. The *Fables* certainly owe something to La Fontaine,* but they are specially adapted to the needs of a particular case. Their moral is always a lesson against pride, vanity, lack of self-control. They condemn flattery and falsehood, and inculcate sincerity, modesty and courage. The *Fables* were followed up by the *Dialogues des Morts* which were composed for the Duke when he was between the ages of twelve and fifteen. They are of course suggested by Lucian's *Dialogues of the Dead*, and Fontenelle had already published in 1683 a work under this title. Fénelon's seventy-nine conversations between pairs of historical (and mythological) characters cover a wide range from Mercury and Charon to Richelieu and Mazarin. But here again history is regarded as a means of conveying moral lessons rather than information, and it is definitely edited for the benefit of the future ruler.

It is, however, in Fénelon's *Télémaque*—a novel with a purpose—that his policy of indirect moral instruction is most vividly illustrated. The book has remained the one item in his vast literary output that has survived. At any rate until quite recent times it formed part of the literary heritage of every French child, and down to the writer's own youth it was an almost indispensable part of the school course for those who were learning French.

* Fénelon also used La Fontaine's own *Fables* and the poet composed several of them especially for the royal pupil—e.g. *Le Chat et les deux Moineaux* and *Le vieux Chat et la jeune Souris*. Book XII of the *Fables* is dedicated to him.

The book was written between 1693 and 1694 and designed primarily for private use in the Duc de Bourgogne's education.* It was composed at odd intervals and at about the same time as the *Dialogues des Morts*. Hence it tends to be somewhat episodic and lacking in shape; but it contains many scenes of much interest and attractively described. Throughout the aim is that of the *Fables* and the *Dialogues*—the moral instruction of the prince who will one day succeed to the throne. The work purports to be a continuation of the fourth book of the *Odyssey*, and it is full of imitations from Homer and Virgil. It describes the adventures of Telemachus in search of his father Odysseus. Under the conduct of Mentor (who is the goddess Minerva in disguise) he goes through a series of adventures which parallel those of Ulysses or Æneas. He travels to many countries and studies different civilisations and governments; and he thus becomes fitted to choose the ideal régime for Ithaca where one day he will be king. The latter part of *Télémaque* deals with a utopian state named Salente, which owes much to the *Republic* of Plato. In the earlier chapters Fénelon had been mainly concerned with lessons of personal morality—for example, pride and idleness are unworthy of a king's son; cowardice and breach of confidence are disgraceful; the tyrant is his own worst enemy. But in describing Salente Fénelon gives expression to some of his most deeply felt political convictions—the king is made for his subjects and not the subjects for the king; war is of all evils the worst; all men are brothers and should love one another. 'Woe to the ungodly who seek a cruel glory in the blood of their brothers, which is really their own blood.'† Agriculture

* It was not published till 1699. See below, p. xlvii.
† *Œuvres*, IV, 267.

and the country life are praised. Life should be simple and luxury should be outlawed, for 'one enriches oneself by despising such riches as exhaust the State, and by reducing one's needs to the bare necessities of life'.*

Like any other novel *Télémaque* is not devoid of a love interest. This is perhaps a little surprising in that its author was a celibate Roman Catholic priest. For this reason Bossuet heartily disapproved of the work. His secretary, the Abbé Le Dieu says in his *Journal*:† 'So many amorous conversations, so many erotic descriptions, a woman who begins the tale by declaring her passion and maintains it to the very end, and all the rest in the same vein, made him comment that this work was unworthy not merely of a bishop, but of a priest and a Christian, and more harmful than profitable to the prince for whom the author had written it.' But Fénelon's experience as superior of the *Nouvelles Catholiques*, and still more as spiritual director to a large number of high-born lady penitents, had obviously given him a considerable insight into feminine psychology and he wished to use this for the advantage of his royal pupil. In *Télémaque* the hero comes successively under the influence of three women of very different types. There is first Calypso who is the counterpart of the seductive enchantress Circe in the *Odyssey*. Her passion for Telemachus and her jealousy of the nymph Eucharis, who has attracted him, are described in vivid terms. 'Her eyes were red and inflamed. There was a gloomy fierceness in her looks which constantly shifted hither and thither. Her cheeks were covered with dark and livid marks and she changed colour every minute. Often she was as pale as death and her tears, which had hitherto flowed in torrents, now ceased—as if rage and despair

* *Œuvres*, IV, 212. † Ed. Guettée (1856), IV, 39.

had dried them up at their source. Scarcely one ran down her cheeks. Her voice became hoarse, tremulous and choked.'* So Calypso represents profane love, but under the influence of Mentor Telemachus resists her wiles. He is however much attracted by Eucharis and her companion nymphs. They represent another type of woman—the charming butterfly, harmless but lacking in real depth of character. So Mentor manages to reason Telemachus out of his passion for her also, though not without regrets on his part. 'I am very conscious', he says, 'of the wound which love has inflicted on me in regard to Eucharis. I can still not pronounce her name without feeling troubled. Time and absence have not enabled me to forget her. But experience has taught me to distrust myself.'† And so he realises that the highest type of love is not just passion, but esteem and appreciation and the regard, respect and affection that will last a lifetime. He will find all this, and much more, in Antiope, who is Fénelon's third type of womanhood.‡ She is his ideal and it is she whom his hero is destined to marry. As Mentor says, 'Vous l'aimez d'un amour raisonnable'.

It was inevitable that *Télémaque* should have been taken by contemporaries, not as a course of instruction for a future king, but as a criticism of the actual régime. The reproaches which Mentor levels at the unreformed ruler Idomeneus are the same as those which are made in the famous letter § in which Fénelon criticises Louis XIV and which was written about the time when *Télémaque* was being composed. It is a tremendous indictment. Fénelon, addressing the king directly, condemns his

* *Œuvres*, IV, 143. † *Ibid.* 330.

‡ See below, pp. 108–10.

§ A translation of this is given in J. McEwen, *Fénelon* (1964), pp. 299–309.

pride and love of flattery, and particularly his military ambitions and extravagance which have brought suffering and ruin upon the whole country. He must learn that the first duty of a monarch is to promote the well-being of his people. All this is put, not as an allegory in a novel or in the form of an examination of conscience for a future ruler, but as a downright condemnation of the king's régime and way of life. 'Your people are dying of hunger; the cultivation of the land is almost abandoned; all trade is languishing; commerce is destroyed. France is nothing but a vast hospital.'* Fénelon strikes even nearer home when he reveals the superficiality of Louis's religion. 'You do not really love God. You merely fear Him with a slave's fear. It is hell that you really fear. Your religion consists simply of superstitions and petty external observances.'† There seems no question about the authenticity of this amazing document, but there is some doubt as to whether it was ever actually seen by the king himself. Viscount St Cyres says: 'Of course the letter was not intended for the King's eye, but for Mme de Maintenon's and Beauvillier's, and Louis's name is only put at the top in order to avoid the inconvenience of addressing severe reproaches directly to them.'‡ Perhaps the problem is not so simple as that. The difficulties are discussed by Paul Janet,§ and more fully by Henri Martin.|| But even if the king never actually saw this document he must have had a shrewd idea of Fénelon's political views. One can at least understand his reaction to *Télémaque*. It is reasonable to suppose that the *Maximes des Saints* was not the only reason why Fénelon was banished to his diocese in 1697.

* *Œuvres*, v, 185. † *Op. cit.* p. 187.
‡ *François de Fénelon* (1901), p. 50. § *Fénelon* (1892), pp. 144–7.
|| *Histoire de France* (1878), xiv, 186–9.

It has already been said that Fénelon's education of the Duc de Bourgogne did not end with his preceptorate and that he continued from afar to supervise the young prince's education as well as he could, and to give him advice on problems of politics and personal conduct. From the year 1701 onwards a whole series of letters passed between the two correspondents. Even during the war in Flanders the contact was kept up, for Fénelon was desperately anxious about the Duke's conduct of the campaign and the current criticisms of his military capacity. These matters are also discussed in a number of letters written to the Duc de Chevreuse 'sur la conduite du Duc de Bourgogne'. It was also in a letter to Chevreuse, dated 27 February 1712, that Fénelon expresses his grief at the Duc de Bourgogne's untimely death. 'God has taken from us our hope for both the Church and the State. He has fashioned this young prince and adorned him and prepared him for a high estate. He has shown him to the world and forthwith taken him from us. I am smitten with horror and ill with the shock, though not through sickness. In lamenting the death of the prince, which breaks my heart, I am alarmed for those still alive. My affection makes me alarmed for you and our good friend the Duc de Beauvillier. Even more I fear for the king whose preservation is of immense importance.'*

Throughout his professional career, from the time when he was appointed superior of the *Nouvelles Catholiques* to the death of the Duc de Bourgogne in 1712, Fénelon was closely concerned with education. In its widest sense it forms the subject of a considerable part of his writings. But, unlike so many of those who have given their views on education to the world, Fénelon

* *Œuvres*, v, 682.

was no mere theorist. In many ways he goes beyond contemporary practice, but he puts his theories to the test, and the results at any rate in the case of the Duc de Bourgogne were to say the least remarkable. Education to Fénelon is never just a matter of acquiring knowledge and technical skills. It implies realising and achieving high standards, whether intellectual, moral or spiritual, and thinking seriously about the major problems and responsibilities which the individual, whatever his particular position in society, has to face. If, as Saint-Simon says, Fénelon was at once the man of letters, the bishop and the great noble, we can surely add that he was one of the greatest educationists of his age, or indeed of any age.

III. *Some bibliographical notes*

The most complete edition of Fénelon's works is that edited by the Sulpician Abbé Gosselin and published between 1820 and 1850. It comprises no less than thirty-five volumes. There are also several smaller collections, and one of the most useful is the *Œuvres de Fénelon* (Paris, 1858). It is from this edition that the references in the present book are quoted. There are also numerous editions of Fénelon's individual works and collections of his letters. The *Œuvres Choisies*, of which there are a number of editions, include all his more important writings.

The classic biography is Cardinal de Bausset's *Histoire de Fénelon*. This was first published in 1808, but there is a four-volume edition, revised and augmented by the Abbé Gosselin, which appeared in 1850. Modern French works dealing with Fénelon include Paul Janet, *Fénelon* (*Les Grands Écrivains Français*, 1892); Jules Lemaître, *Fénelon* (1910); Albert Delplanque, *La Pensée de Fénelon*

(1930); Maxime Leroy, *Fénelon* (*Reformateurs Sociaux*, 1928); Emmanuel de Broglie, *Fénelon à Cambrai* (1884). In English *François de Fénelon* by Viscount St Cyres (1901) is a most able and interesting study; and Miss E. K. Sanders's *Fénelon, his Friends and Enemies* (1901) is also very useful. The Mme Guyon episode is attractively dealt with in Michael de la Bedoyere's *The Archbishop and the Lady* (1956), and a selection of Fénelon's letters, translated by Sir John McEwen, has recently (1964) become available. For shorter accounts of Fénelon's life and work the reader may be referred to chapter VIII in Arthur Tilley's *Decline of the Age of Louis XIV* (1929), and Mr R. A. Jones's article (pp. 70–103) in *The Social and Political Ideas of some great French Thinkers of the Age of Reason* (ed. Hearnshaw, 1930). There is also some interesting material on Fénelon's theological views in W. H. Jervis, *History of the Church of France* (1872), vol. II, chapter III. Many of the matters dealt with in the present work are discussed in greater detail in my *The French Tradition in Education* (1922), *Mme de Maintenon and Saint-Cyr* (1934), and *Girls at School under the Ancien Régime* (1954).

The *Traité de l'Éducation des Filles*, which was first published in 1687, has passed through a large number of editions and received the attention of many distinguished French educationists. Editions of this treatise were issued by Paul Rousselot in 1883 and by Octave Gréard in 1890. The book was soon translated into English. In 1707 there appeared *Instructions for the Education of a Daughter, by the Author of Telemachus, done into English and revised by Dr George Hickes*. Several other editions of the work were issued during the course of the eighteenth century. In 1805 an author named Dibdin produced a translation of the treatise 'adapted to English readers'; and in 1841 *The Education of Daughters* by M. B. was published in Dublin. *The Accomplished Governess abridg'd from a dissertation by the Author of Telemachus* (1752) is a hash-up of the final chapter of Fénelon's treatise. As will be seen, most of these English versions were 'revised' or 'adapted to English readers' or 'abridged'. An example of what this implied is afforded by Dr Hickes's translation. The writer, who has merited five pages in the *Dictionary of National Biography*, was an Oxford Doctor of Divinity. He was penalised by James II for resisting the Declaration of Indulgence and by William and Mary for refusing the oath of allegiance. He became bishop of Thetford and his attitude to Fénelon's book therefore is that of a Protestant ecclesiastic. In order not to offend the susceptibilities of his readers, and in an attempt to bring Fénelon's book into harmony with the eighteenth-century attitude of the Church of England, the translator does not scruple to insert, not merely short phrases or sentences of his own, but even passages of several pages in length. On the other hand he ruthlessly suppresses or distorts any reference which has a definitely Roman Catholic flavour. For example, such subjects as confession, extreme unction, and the 'religious' life disappear altogether or are replaced by edifying remarks of a distinctly Protestant character. Moreover, there is added to Hickes's translation (or adaptation) a sort of supplement, addressed to a great lady under the pseudonym of Antiope.* This is a kind of imitation of Fénelon's *Avis à une Dame de Qualité*, and it is entitled *Institutions for a Young Princess, or The Idea of a Lady of Honour*. This is followed by *Instructions for a Governess according to the Model of the Lord Archbishop of Cambray*;

* This name was taken from *Télémaque*. See below, pp. 108–10.

and it is in fact a summary of chapter XIII of Fénelon's treatise. The work ends with a number of 'Devotions' and a short *Office for a Governess*, with prayers for the use of a young lady 'according to the Discretion and Capacity and Age of the Person instructed'. It can be seen then that the Hickes's translation, although in vogue in this country for nearly a hundred years, gives only a garbled idea of what Fénelon really said and what he intended. It ignores the fact that he was a Roman Catholic cleric, and it interlards his recommendations with instructions which may, or may not, be appropriate but which were no part of Fénelon's own work. Moreover there is never the slightest indication of what is owed to the author himself and what are the translator's additions or adaptations.

It has been said above that the *Traité de l'Éducation des Filles* was composed at the request of the Duchesse de Beauvillier. She had married the Duke in 1671 and they had thirteen children of whom nine were girls. The eldest died in infancy, and one married her cousin, the Duc de Mortemont; but the other seven all became nuns. The treatise was written about 1685, though it was not actually published till 1687. In the 1715 reprint, however, there was annexed to the original work an *Avis à une Dame de Qualité sur l'Éducation de Mademoiselle sa Fille.* It seems usually assumed that this 'Dame de Qualité' is the same as the lady for whom the original *Traité* was composed—that is, the Duchesse de Beauvillier.* But as she was aged eighteen at the time of her marriage in 1671 it seems likely that her educational responsibilities to her children were over by the time that the *Avis* appeared—though, of course, it might have

* See, for example, Rousselot, *Histoire de l'Éducation des Femmes en France* (1883), I, 385 n.

been written earlier, for Fénelon died in 1715. However, it says quite definitely at the beginning of this document that the lady to whom it is addressed has 'only one single daughter to bring up'. But in any case the *Avis* is in essence a précis of what Fénelon had already said in his *Traité*, though it emphasises in particular the risks of conventual education and the advantages of bringing a girl up at home, so long as her mother takes her responsibilities seriously. It seems unlikely that, having already dealt at length with the education of girls for the benefit of the Duchesse de Beauvillier in his original treatise, Fénelon should simply repeat his advice at her request in the *Avis*.

Of Fénelon's other works *Télémaque* has had an even more conspicuous career than the *Traité*. Composed between 1694 and 1696 in connection with the Duc de Bourgogne's education, it was published, incompletely and without Fénelon's consent, at the Hague in 1699. The first authentic edition, 'conforme au manuscrit original', was issued under the direction of Fénelon's great nephew, the Marquis de Fénelon, in 1717—two years after the author's death. It became immediately, and has remained, immensely popular. The *Bibliothèque Nationale* catalogue lists no less than 516 editions and reprints of *Télémaque* in French, not counting selections and abridgments. The work was also translated into practically every European language, not to mention Breton, Armenian, Latin and modern Greek. The first English version appeared in 1742, and many more were published during the eighteenth century. The book was even rendered into English verse.

The provenance of the document which illustrates the education of the Duc de Bourgogne, and a translation of which appears on pp. 111–18, requires a little explanation.

It is ultimately the work of Charles Auguste d'Allonville, Marquis de Louville, about whom something must be said. He belonged to a noble family of Champagne and was educated first by an uncle who was an ardent Jansenist and afterwards at a Jesuit *collège*. From the one he imbibed 'une religion austère et solide', and from the other 'une respectueuse submission aux décisions de l'église'. After service in the army he became friendly with the Duc and Duchesse de Beauvillier, and through them was associated with the religious coterie at the French court to which they belonged and in which Fénelon played so important a part. In 1689 De Beauvillier had been appointed *gouverneur* to the Duc de Bourgogne and Fénelon became his *précepteur*. But in the following year the Dauphin's second son, the Duc d'Anjou, also left the care of a governess, and De Louville was attached to his suite as a *gentilhomme de la manche*.* Later the youngest brother, the Duc de Berry, joined the group. Thus the education of the three boys largely overlapped and was under the general direction of De Beauvillier and Fénelon.

When in 1700 the Duc d'Anjou became King of Spain De Louville accompanied him as *gentilhomme de sa chambre*. He subsequently returned to France and was appointed to a similar position in the household of the Duc de Bourgogne. He wrote some *Mémoires Secrets* which are largely concerned with the establishment of the House of Bourbon in Spain. But they also contain an account of the education which the three sons of the Dauphin had received in their boyhood under the direc-

* A note in Bausset, *Histoire de Fénelon*, I, 163, says: 'On appeloit alors *gentilshommes de la manche* ceux qui, à raison du service assidu qu'ils devoient à un prince, étoient habituellement à ses côtés, et comme *à sa manche*.' We might say that they were always 'at their master's elbow'.

tion of De Beauvillier and Fénelon. These *Mémoires* were edited by the Marquis du Roure, and extracts from them are also quoted at some length in Bausset's *Histoire de Fénelon.** Bausset considers that the date of the memorandum is 1696 when the Duc de Bourgogne was fourteen, the Duc d'Anjou thirteen, and the Duc de Berry ten. The two accounts in some measure overlap, but each also contains material not included in the other. In order, therefore, to give as complete a picture as possible, I have ventured to conflate the two documents.

* I, 244–50.

Superior figures in the translations refer to the Notes which will be found on pp. 134–44.

THE EDUCATION OF GIRLS

CHAPTER I

The importance of the education of girls

Nothing is more neglected than the education of girls. Custom and the caprice of mothers often decide the whole matter. People imagine that this sex should be given little instruction. The education of boys is regarded as a most important matter because of its bearing on the public weal; and although almost as many mistakes are made in it as in the education of girls, we are at least given to understand that to carry it out successfully much intelligence is needed. Persons of the highest attainments[1] have devoted themselves to laying down rules for this subject. How many masters and colleges[2] do we see! What sums are spent on printing books, on learned researches, on methods of learning languages,[3] on the choice of teachers! All these steps are often more apparent than real; but they do show the high idea that we have of the education of boys. As for girls, it is said, there is no need for them to be learned; curiosity makes them vain and affected; it is enough for them to know how one day to look after their households and obey their husbands without asking why. Reference is invariably made to the numerous women whose intellectual attainments have made them ridiculous. After that it is thought justifiable to hand girls over blindly to the guidance of ignorant and foolish mothers.

We should certainly beware of making blue-stockings. A woman's intellect is normally more feeble and her curiosity greater than those of a man; also it is undesirable to set her to studies which may turn her head. Women should not govern the state or make war or enter the sacred ministry.[4] Thus they can dispense with some of the more difficult branches of knowledge which deal with politics, the military art, jurisprudence, philosophy and theology. Even the majority of the mechanical arts are not suitable to them. They are made for exercise in moderation. Their bodies as well as their minds are less strong and robust than those of men. On the other hand, nature has given them as a recompense industry, neatness and economy, so as to keep them quietly occupied in their homes.

But what results from this natural weakness of women? The weaker they are the more important it is to strengthen them. Have they not duties to fulfil—duties which are fundamental in all human life? Is it not women who ruin or sustain their homes, who regulate every detail of domestic life and therefore decide what touches the human race most nearly? That is why they affect most closely the good or bad habits of practically all mankind. A wise, diligent and religious woman is the soul of a great house; she orders its temporal affairs and its eternal salvation. Even men who hold high authority in public affairs cannot by their deliberations effect any useful reform if women do not help them to carry it out.

The world is not an abstraction; it is the sum total of families; and who can civilise it more effectively than women who, in addition to their natural authority and assiduity in the household, have the advantage of being by nature careful, attentive to detail, industrious, attractive and persuasive? But can men hope to obtain any happiness in life if their most intimate association—that of marriage—is turned into bitterness? And what will become of the children, who are destined to be the human race of the next generation, if their mothers spoil them from their earliest years?

Such then are the duties of women, and they are scarcely less important to the public than those of men, since women have a household to rule, a husband to make happy, and children to bring up well. Add to this that virtue is as necessary to women as it is to men. To say nothing of the good or the harm that they can do to society, they form half of the human race redeemed by the blood of Jesus Christ and destined to eternal life.

In short, one has to consider not only the good which women do when they are well brought up, but also the evil which they cause in the world when they lack an education which inspires them to virtue. It is unquestionable that bad education does more harm in the case of women than in that of men, since the failings of men are often due to the bad education which they have received from their mothers and from the passions which other women inspire in them at a later age.

How often does history show us intrigues,[5] subversions of law and morality, sanguinary wars, innovations in religion, revolutions in government—all due to the profligacy of women! That illustrates the importance of bringing up girls well. Let us see how it is to be done.

CHAPTER II

Disadvantages of ordinary education

Ignorance is the reason for a girl being bored and not knowing how to occupy herself. When she gets to a certain age without developing serious interests she cannot acquire either the taste for them or an appreciation of them. Whatever is serious seems dismal to her; whatever calls for continued application makes her tired; the inclination to pleasure, which is strong in youth, the example of others of the same age who are given over to amusement—all this serves to make her dread a well-regulated and industrious life. At this early age she lacks the experience and the authority for sharing in the administration of her parents' household. She does not even realise the importance of giving her mind to this, unless her mother has taken the trouble to put her in touch with its details. If she is high-born she is exempt from manual work; she will work therefore only for an hour or so every day, and just because people say—without knowing why—that it is proper for women to work; but often it will be only a sham and she will not accustom herself to steady work.

That being so, what will be her condition? She is bored and put off by the company of a mother who watches her and scolds her, who thinks to bring her up well by never pardoning her, who compromises with her, who puts up with her whims, who seems always weighed down by domestic cares. She is surrounded by women who flatter her and try to win her favour by ignoble and dangerous complacency, who gratify all her fancies and entertain her with everything that will make her dislike the good. Piety seems to her a tedious business and inimical to pleasure. With what then will she occupy herself? With nothing useful. This lack of application even develops into an incurable habit.

Here then is a great want that one cannot hope to fill with serious interests. Frivolous ones must therefore take their place. Having nothing to do the girl abandons herself to idleness; and idleness is a weakness of the soul,[6] an inexhaustible source of boredom. She gets into the habit of sleeping a third longer than is necessary for the preservation of perfect health. This long sleep serves only to weaken her, to make her more delicate, more liable to bodily disturbances; whereas sleep in moderation, joined with regular exercise, keeps a person cheerful, vigorous and healthy. This undoubtedly makes for bodily perfection, to say nothing of the advantages which the soul gains.

When this softness and indolence are joined to ignorance there results a dangerous inclination towards amusements and entertainments. This indeed it is which excites an indiscreet and insatiable curiosity. Those who are well-educated and occupied in serious pursuits have as a rule only a moderate curiosity. That which they know gives them a disdain for many things of which they are ignorant. They see the uselessness and folly of most of those subjects which small-minded people, who know nothing and have nothing to do, are eager to learn.

On the other hand, girls who are badly educated and indolent have an imagination which is always straying. Lacking solid nourishment their curiosity turns eagerly towards vain and dangerous objects. Those who have intelligence often develop into blue-stockings[7] and read every book which can feed their vanity. They develop a passion for novels,[8] for plays, for fanciful tales of adventure with a romantic love interest. They give way to empty ideas and grow accustomed to the high-flown language of the heroes of fiction. By so doing they even spoil themselves for ordinary life, for all these fine, but airy, sentiments, these noble passions, these adventures which the fiction-writer invents in order to please, have no relation to the motives which hold sway in real life and which decide actual events, nor to the disappointments which one meets in whatever one takes in hand.

An unhappy girl, full of the romance and wonder which have fascinated her in these books, is astonished to find in the world no real people who are like these heroes. She longs to live like these imaginary princesses who in novels are always charming, always worshipped, always independent. How she will hate to descend from this romance to the sordid details of housekeeping!

Some girls push their curiosity still further and take upon themselves to express opinions on religious matters, although they are incapable of doing so. But those who have insufficient intellectual aptitude for these curiosities, still have others proportionate to their powers. They are eager to know what is said—a story, a rumour, an intrigue. They like to receive letters and to read those which others receive. They want to be told everything and to tell everything. They are vain and vanity makes them talkative. They are frivolous and their frivolity prevents the reflection which would often help them to keep silence.

CHAPTER III

The foundations of education

In order to remedy these evils it is a great advantage to be able to begin the education of girls from their earliest childhood. This first stage, which is entrusted to indiscreet—and sometimes ill-conducted—women, is none the less that in which the most marked impressions are made and which therefore has great influence on all the rest of one's life.

Even before children have learnt to speak properly they can be prepared for instruction. It may be thought that I claim too much, but one has only to consider what the child is doing who as yet cannot speak. He is learning a language which he will soon speak more fluently than the learned, at a riper age, can speak the dead languages which they have studied with so much assiduity. What do we mean by learning a language? It is not simply committing to memory a large number of words. It is rather, as St Augustine says, noticing the meaning of each of these separate words. 'The child,' he says, 'amid his crying and playing is noticing of what object each word is the sign. Sometimes he does this by considering the natural bodily movements which touch or point to objects of which one speaks; sometimes he is struck by the frequent repetition of the same word for describing the same object. It is true that the mental constitution of children is particularly adapted to the impression of such images. But what intellectual concentration is needed to distinguish them and to associate each with its object!'

Consider again how children at this early age are attracted to those who indulge them and avoid those who thwart them; how well they know when to cry or to be silent in order to get what they want; how full they are of tricks and jealousy. 'I have seen', says St Augustine, 'a jealous child who could not speak, and yet already looked with a pale face and angry eyes at the other child who hung at the breast with him.' We can conclude, then, that children understand at an earlier age than is generally realised. Thus you can give them by words, aided by the tone of your voice or by gestures, the desire to be with the good and virtuous people whom they see rather than with others who are not reasonable and whom it would be dangerous for them to love. Thus by the different expressions of your face or by the tone of your voice you can express your horror at people whom they have seen giving way to anger or any other evil passion, and assume the mildest tone and the most serene expression to show them your admiration for wise and modest conduct.

I am not exaggerating insignificant matters. These early dispositions are a beginning which must not be neglected, and this method of preparing children in good time has imperceptible effects which render education more easy. If there is still any doubt as to the influence which these early childish predilections have on the adult, we have but to consider how often the remembrance of things which one liked in childhood is still vivid and effective in mature age. If instead of giving children stupid fears of ghosts and spirits, which cannot but agitate and weaken their still undeveloped minds; if instead of letting them follow all the fancies of their nurses as to the things they should seek after or avoid, we were to aim at always giving them an attractive idea of the good and a terrifying idea of evil, this tendency would greatly help them to practise all the virtues for the future. As things are they are made to dread a priest who is dressed in black; death is never mentioned to them except to frighten them; they are told that the dead come back at night in horrible guise. The only result of all this is to make them weak and timid, and to prejudice them against better things.

The most useful course in the earliest years of infancy is to look after the child's health, to try to keep his blood pure by a careful choice of food and by a simple régime. His meals must be so arranged that he has them as far as possible always at the same times; that they are sufficiently frequent, according to his needs; that he does not eat between meals, because this overloads the stomach while digestion is not yet completed; that he eats nothing highly spiced which would stimulate him to eat more than he needs and would make him dislike food more suited to his health; and finally that he is not given too many kinds of food, for a variety of dishes, one after the other, stimulates the appetite after the real need for food is satisfied.

A still more important point is to let the bodily organs grow strong without overdoing their development; to avoid anything which may excite the passions; to inure the child gradually to doing without things for which he has shown too much eagerness, so that he may not always expect to get what he wants.

Though children are naturally but little inclined towards the good, yet they can by these means be made obedient, patient, strong, happy, serene. But if they are neglected from their earliest years they become passionate and restless all their life long. Their blood is inflamed and habits are formed. Their bodies, which are still tender, and their souls, which have as yet no definite tendencies, begin to incline towards evil. In them a kind of second original sin is conceived which is the source of endless irregularities when they are older.

As soon as they have reached a more advanced age, when their reasoning powers are more fully developed, it is essential that whatever is said to them should serve to make them love truth and inspire them with a disdain for any kind of pretence. One should therefore never have recourse to any deceit in order to silence them or to impress one's wishes upon them. In that way they are taught a cunning which they never forget; they must be led by reason as far as possible.

But let us examine more closely the condition of children so as to see in detail what is suitable for them. Their brain substance is soft[9] and hardens gradually; as for their mind, it knows nothing and finds everything new. The result of this softness of the brain is that everything is easily impressed on it and the surprise of novelty makes children quickly moved to admiration and extremely curious. It is true also that this moistness and softness of the brain, together with a great heat, give rise to facile and continual movement. This is the cause of that constant activity of children, for they cannot concentrate their attention on any object nor keep their body still in any one place.

On the other hand, since children are as yet quite unable to think or act for themselves, they notice everything and say little unless they are made accustomed to talking—and that is to be carefully guarded against. Often the pleasure which one hopes to derive from lively children spoils them. We get them into the way of risking whatever comes into their heads and to speak about things of which they have as yet no definite knowledge. They retain for the rest of their lives the habit of judging without reflection and of saying things about which they have no clear ideas; and this produces a very bad mental disposition. This pleasure which we hope to derive from children has an even worse effect. They see that we regard them with complacency, that we notice everything that they do, that we listen to them with pleasure. And so they get into the habit of thinking that the world will always be interested in them.

During this period when they are praised and have not as yet experienced any contradiction they conceive empty hopes which are destined to bring them endless disappointments all their life long. I have seen children who think that we are talking about them every time we speak secretly, because they have noticed that we have often done this. They imagine that they have no characteristics but such as are unusual and admirable. It is necessary therefore to take care of children without letting them realise that we are thinking much about them. Show them that it is out of kindness and the need which they have to be corrected that you are watchful of their conduct, and not out of admiration for their cleverness. Be content to mould them gradually, according to the opportunities which present themselves in the ordinary course. Even when you could greatly advance a child's intellectual development without pressing him, you should shrink from doing so; for the danger of vanity and pertness is always greater than the fruits of these premature educations about which so much fuss is made.

We must then be content to follow and to aid nature.[10] Children know little. They must not be over-stimulated to talk, but as they are ignorant of many things they have many questions to ask—and so they ask many. It is enough to answer them definitely and sometimes to add some little comparison which may make more obvious the explanations which one gives them. If they pass judgment on something without proper knowledge of it, we should puzzle them by some fresh question, so as to make them realise their fault without abashing them roughly. At the same time we should make them realise, not by vague praises but by some definite mark of approval, that we are much more pleased with them when they are in doubt and ask about what they do not know, than when they make the best decisions of which they themselves are capable. This is the most effective and politest way of instilling into their minds true modesty, together with a great contempt for the disputes which are so characteristic of ignorant young people.

As soon as their reason appears to have made some progress you should avail yourself of this experience to warn them against pride. You will see—you will say—

that you are better able to reason now than you were a year ago; in a year's time you will see things which you are not able to see today. If you had wished a year ago to pass judgment on things which you know now but did not know then, you would have judged badly. You would have made a great mistake in pretending to know what was beyond your reach. It is the same today with the things which remain for you to know. You will see one day how imperfect your present judgments are. Meanwhile you can trust the advice of those who judge as you yourself will judge when you have reached their age and had their experience.

Childish curiosity is a natural tendency which, as it were, leads to instruction. Do not fail to profit by it. For example, in the country they see a mill and they want to know what it is. You should show them how the food on which they live is prepared. They see the reapers, and you should explain what they are doing—how the corn is sown and how it grows in the earth. In the town they see shops where various businesses are carried on and where different kinds of goods are sold. One should never be wearied by their questions; these are opportunities which nature offers you to facilitate their instruction. Show that you are pleased by them; in so doing you will imperceptibly teach them the various processes which are of service to man and upon which commerce depends. Gradually, and without special study, they will learn the right way of doing what is useful to them and the proper price of each thing—and that is the true basis of housekeeping. This knowledge which no one should despise, since we should all avoid being cheated, is particularly necessary for girls.

CHAPTER IV

Imitation to beware of

The ignorance of children, on whose brains no impressions have as yet been made and who have acquired no habits, makes them impressionable and inclined to imitate everything that they see. That is why it is of the first importance to give them none but the best examples. Only those people should be allowed access to them whose examples are useful to follow; but since it is inevitable that, in spite of the precautions which are taken, they will see many irregularities, they must early be made to realise the impropriety of those who are vicious and irrational, whose reputation does not admit of any excuse. They should be shown how often one is despised—or worthy of being so, how often one is miserable when one gives way to one's passions and does not cultivate one's reason. In this way without accustoming them to being laughed at you can form their taste and make them appreciative of those things which are truly becoming. You should not even refrain from giving them some warning in general terms against certain faults, even though by so doing you risk opening their eyes to the weaknesses of people whom they ought to respect. For in addition to the fact that you should not expect—and it is not right—to keep them in ignorance of the true rules on this matter, the most sure means of holding them to their duty is to persuade them that one should put up with other people's faults and not even pass judgment on these hastily, that they often seem greater than they really are, that they are outweighed by good qualities and that, as nothing on this earth is perfect, one should admire that which has least imperfections. In short, even though such admonitions should be kept as a last resource, one should none the less give children the right principles and restrain them from imitating all the evil which they have before their eyes.

You should also prevent them from imitating silly people, for their mocking and farcical ways have in them something vulgar and contrary to decent feeling. One must beware of children picking up these habits, because the vividness of their imagination and their bodily activity, together with their playfulness, lead them easily to adopt all sorts of attitudes in order to imitate the ridiculous things which they see. Children's tendency to imitate leads to infinite harm when they are entrusted to people lacking in virtue, who scarcely restrain themselves in their company. But God by giving children this inclination has afforded them a means of turning easily towards whatever good is shown to them. Often, without saying a word to them, you have only to let them see in someone else what you want them to do.

CHAPTER V

Indirect instruction. Children should not be forced

I even believe that you should often make use of indirect instruction,[11] which is not wearisome like set lessons or reproaches, in order simply to arouse their attention to the examples which are set before them.

Someone might ask someone else in their hearing 'Why are you doing that?' The other might answer 'I am doing it for such and such a reason'. For example:

'Why did you acknowledge your fault?' 'Because I should have committed a greater one if I had denied it like a coward by telling a lie; and there is nothing finer than saying frankly "I was in the wrong".' After that the first person could praise the other who had thus accused himself. But it is essential that all this should be done without any affectation, for children are much more knowing than one thinks; and if once they have perceived some trick on the part of those who look after them, they lose the simplicity and confidence which nature gave them.

We have pointed out that in children the brain is altogether warm and moist, and that this causes them to be continually in motion. This softness of the brain allows everything to be easily impressed on it and renders very vivid the images of all objects which are perceived. So we must hasten to write on their brains[12] while the characters can be easily formed there. But we must be careful in choosing the images which should be inscribed, for we should store up in a receptacle so small and so precious only the choicest things. We must remember to preserve in their minds at this age only what we hope will remain there all their life long. The first images inscribed on the brain while it is still soft and where nothing as yet has been written are the most deeply impressed. Moreover they grow harder as the brain gets drier with age, and so they become indelible. That is why when one is old one often remembers distinctly the events of one's youth, far removed though they be; whereas one can remember less about those things which happened when one was older because the impressions were made on the brain when it was already dry and full of other images.

When one hears this kind of argument it is difficult

to believe it. It is none the less true that one reasons without even being aware of it. Do we not often hear it said 'I have become fixed; I am too old to change; I was brought up like that'? Again, do we not take a singular pleasure in recalling the memories of childhood, and are not the strongest inclinations those which were acquired at that age? Does not all this prove that the earliest impressions and the earliest habits are the strongest? If childhood is the right time to inscribe images on the brain it must be confessed that it is least suited for the exercise of reason. This moistness of the brain which makes impressions easy, joined with great warmth, produces an activity which prevents continued application.

A child's brain is like a lighted candle in a windy place. Its light is always flickering. A child asks you a question and, before you can answer, his eyes are raised to the ceiling and he is counting the figures which are painted there or the panes of glass which form the window. If you try to bring him back to his original topic you cause him as much annoyance as if you kept him in prison. So you must humour his weaknesses carefully and wait till he gets stronger. Reply at once to his question and let him ask as many more as he likes. Simply keep his curiosity alive and gather in his memory a store of good materials. The time will come when they will accumulate of themselves and when the child will begin to reason because his brain has more solidity. Content yourself with setting him right when he reasons incorrectly and make him realise, without haste and according to the opportunities which he will afford you, what it means to form a correct judgment.

Let the child, then, play and mingle instruction with games. Let wisdom reveal herself to him, but gradually and with a smiling face. Beware of tiring him by an excessive strictness.

If a child gets a sad and forbidding idea of virtue, if liberty and licence are shown to him in attractive guise, all is lost; your labour is in vain. Never let him be flattered by mean-spirited or ill-conducted persons. We grow accustomed to love the manners and ideas of those whom we love. If we derive pleasure from dishonourable people, we shall eventually come little by little to approve even of that which is despicable in them.

In order to make children fond of good people help them to realise their attractive and pleasant qualities—their sincerity, modesty, unselfishness, reliability, discreetness, and above all their piety, which is the source of all the other qualities. But if anyone of this type has a failing you should say: 'Piety is not the cause of faults like that. When it is perfect it removes them or at any rate mitigates them.' After all, we need not insist on making children admire certain pious folk whose appearance is by no means attractive.

Even though you watch your own conduct so that nothing but good can be seen, do not expect that the child will never discern any faults in you. Often he will notice even your smallest failings. St Augustine tells us that from his early childhood he had noticed the vanity of his masters in respect of their attainments. The best and most urgent thing for you to do is to realise your own failings—the more so as the child will realise them—and get some sincere friends to warn you of them. As a rule those who have charge of children never forgive them anything, but they forgive themselves everything. This arouses in children a critical and hostile spirit so that when they see that the person who has charge of them has committed some fault they are delighted and seek only to condemn it.

Avoid this difficulty. Never be afraid to speak of the faults which are apparent in yourself and of those which have escaped you in the child's presence. If you see that he is capable of understanding reason tell him that you want to set him an example of correcting his faults by correcting your own. By so doing you can derive even from your own imperfections a means of instructing and edifying the child; you will even avoid the scorn and dislike for yourself which your faults may give him.

At the same time you should seek every means of making pleasant to the child the things which you demand of him. If you have something distasteful to propose make him understand that the pain will soon be followed by pleasure. Show him always the usefulness of the things which you teach him. Make him see their value in reference to ordinary affairs and the duties of society. Without that, study may seem to him an abstract, barren and unattractive toil. 'What's the good', the child will say to himself, 'of learning all these things which are never mentioned in conversation and have no reference to anything which one has to do?' You must therefore give him a reason for everything that you teach. You will say to him: 'My object is to help you to do what you will have to do one day, to form your judgment, to accustom you to reason well on all the problems of life.' You should always set before him a fixed and pleasant aim which will help him in his work, and never expect to hold him in subjection by a harsh and absolute authority. In proportion as children's reason develops you should reason with them more and more as to what is necessary in their education, not in order to follow their inclinations but to profit by it when they realise their true condition, to test their powers of discernment, and to give them a taste for the things which you want them to do.

Never, unless it is absolutely necessary, assume a severe and commanding air which makes children afraid. This is often a sign of affectation and pedantry on the part of educators, for children are as a rule only too timid and bashful. You will shut up their hearts and lose their confidence, without which no results can be expected in education. Make yourself loved by them. Let them be quite often with you and never afraid to let you see their faults. To achieve that be lenient towards those who are frank with you. Do not appear shocked or annoyed by their evil tendencies; on the contrary be sympathetic with their weakness. Sometimes there may result the disadvantage that they will be less restrained by fear; but, when all is said, confidence and sincerity are more helpful to them than stern authority.

None the less you will have to resort to authority if confidence and persuasion are not sufficiently strong. But you should always begin by being frank, pleasant and affable—though not familiar; this will enable you to see the child acting naturally and to understand him thoroughly. In short, even though you should compel him by your authority to observe all your rules you would still not achieve your aim. Everything would degenerate into wearisome formalities, and perhaps into hypocrisy. You would make the child hate the good when you ought to seek solely to inspire him with a love of it.

If the Wise Man[13] always recommends parents to have the rod in readiness for their children, if he says that a father who sports with his son will weep hereafter, this does not mean that he blames a gentle and patient education. He is simply condemning those slack and thoughtless parents who pander to their children's weaknesses and who do not try to wean them from these in their earliest years, and even go so far as to put up with all sorts of extremes. We must conclude then that parents should always preserve the authority to punish, for there are some natures which must be tamed by fear; but it must be repeated that this should be done only when no other way is possible.

A child who is still swayed by his imagination and who gets a confused impression of the things which are presented to him in a mass, hates study and virtue because he has already conceived an aversion for the person who speaks to him about them. That is why there arises this dreary and repulsive conception of piety which the child retains all his life long; it is often all that remains to him of a stern upbringing. Often you should put up with things which ought to be corrected and wait for the moment when the child's mind is ready to profit by correction. Never rebuke him either at his first impulse or at your own. If you do it at your own he will realise that you are acting in a temper and in a hurry, and are not actuated by reason and kindness. You will lose your authority beyond recall. If you rebuke him at his first impulse his mind is not free enough to acknowledge his fault, to overcome his passion and to realise the importance of your advice. You risk making the child lose the respect which he owes you. Let him always see that you are master of yourself; nothing will make him realise that better than your patience. If it is necessary, notice his behaviour for several days, so as to correct him at the best possible opportunity. Never speak to a child about his fault without pointing out some way of overcoming it and so encouraging him to do this; for you should beware of the disappointment and frustration which arise from correction when it is harsh. If you find that a child is somewhat amenable to reason I think that he should be encouraged imperceptibly to ask that he should be told of his faults. This is the way to tell him of them without distressing him. Never tell him of several faults at the same time.

It should be remembered that the child's mind is undeveloped, that his age makes him still attracted only by pleasure, and that he is often expected to show a strictness and seriousness of which those who demand them are themselves not capable. We even make a dangerous impression of boredom and annoyance on the child's mind by talking to him of words and things not one of which he can understand; no liberty, no cheerfulness—nothing but lessons, silence, uncomfortable postures, punishments, threats. The ancients understood this matter far better. It was through the pleasures of poetry and music that the chief branches of knowledge, the maxims of virtue and of civilisation, were introduced among the Hebrews, the Egyptians and the Greeks. Uneducated people can scarcely believe that, so far removed is it from our own customs. Yet a very small knowledge of history shows beyond doubt that this was the ordinary practice for many centuries. Let us at least in our days limit ourselves to mingling the pleasant with the useful as far as we can.[14]

Although we can hardly hope to avoid completely the use of fear in the case of most children, whose nature is stubborn and intractable, yet we should not have recourse to it until we have patiently tried all other remedies. Children must always be made to understand clearly what it is that is asked of them and what it is that will please you. For joy and confidence should be their ordinary nature; otherwise their spirit is weakened and their courage dashed. If they are active we irritate them; if they are sluggish we make them stupid. Fear is like the violent remedies which are applied in serious diseases; they purge, but they change the state of the body and stimulate the organs. If a soul is directed by fear it is always the weaker for it.

For the rest, although you should not be always threatening without punishing, for fear of your threats being despised, yet you should punish less than you threaten. As for punishments, the pain should be as light as possible, but accompanied with all the circumstances which may affect the child with shame and remorse. For example, show him all that you have done to avoid going to extremes; show him that you are sorry about it; speak to others in his presence about the unhappiness of those who are so lacking in reason and honour that they have to be punished; restrict the ordinary marks of kindness until you see that the child needs to be comforted; make the punishment public or private, according as you consider it will be most helpful to the child either by making him thoroughly ashamed or by showing him that he has been spared. Keep a public disgrace as the last resort; get the help sometimes of a discreet person who will console the child and tell him what you yourself should not as yet tell him, who will cure him of his false shame and dispose him to return to you, and to whom the child, in his emotion, can open his heart more freely than he dares do before you. But above all let the child see that you never ask of him submission unless it is absolutely necessary. Try to get him to condemn himself and to do it with a good grace, so that all that remains for you is to lessen the pain which he will have accepted. These general rules must be applied according to the needs of particular cases.

Men—and particularly children—are not always the same. What is good today may be dangerous tomorrow, and a treatment which never varies cannot be useful.

The less formal lessons are the better. An enormous amount of information, more useful than lessons themselves, can be introduced in the course of cheerful conversation. I have known several children who learnt reading as a game.[15] You have but to tell them interesting stories, taken in their presence from a book, and make them learn their letters imperceptibly. After that they will be eager to gain the power of going of themselves to the source of that which gives them pleasure.

There are two things which spoil it all—that they are made to read at first in Latin[16] (and this takes from them all the pleasure of reading), and that we try to get them into the habit of reading with a forced and ridiculous emphasis. The child should be given a well-bound book, with a gilt binding if possible, with attractive pictures and clear print. Whatever pleases the imagination facilitates study. You should choose a book containing short and interesting tales. If you do this you need not be afraid that the child will not learn to read. But do not worry him by making him read exactly; let him pronounce naturally, as he speaks. Other kinds of intonation are always wrong and suggest a college declamation. As soon as his tongue is loosened, his chest strengthened, and he has had some practice in reading, he will read without difficulty, with more expression and more distinctly.

The method of teaching writing is much the same. When once children have learnt to read a little they may be allowed as an amusement to form their letters; and if there are several children together you can introduce emulation. Children are of themselves given to draw on paper. However little you assist this inclination, if you do not tire them too much, they will form their letters for the fun of doing so and gradually accustom themselves to write. You may even encourage them to do so by promising as a reward something which they like and which has no dangerous results. 'Write me a letter', you will say. 'Send this message to your brother or your cousin.' That pleases the child provided that he is not troubled with the unattractive idea of a regular lesson. Untrammelled curiosity, says St Augustine out of his own experience, develops a child's intellect far more effectively than a rule or a necessity imposed by fear.

Notice a great fault in ordinary education. All the pleasure is put on one side and all the irksomeness on the other—all the irksomeness in study and all the pleasure in amusements. What can the child do but endure authority impatiently and then run off eagerly to his play? Try to reverse this state of affairs. Make study attractive; conceal it under the guise of freedom and pleasure. Let children vary their studies from time to time by little turns of amusement. They need these diversions in order to refresh their minds. Let their eyes roam a little; even allow them occasionally some distraction or game so as to ease their minds; then bring them back gently to the matter in hand. To insist too strictly on their studying without relaxation often does them much harm. Those who have charge of children often insist on this strictness because it suits them better than to have to profit by opportunities as they occur. At the same time banish from children's games whatever raises their passions too much; but offer them as an attractive change whatever can refresh their minds, satisfy their curiosity about useful things, and exercise their bodies in suitable occupations. All this should form part of children's amusements. The ones they like best are those in which the body is in motion. So long as they can be continually moving from place to place they are happy; a shuttlecock or a ball is all that is needed. Thus there is no necessity to worry about their amusements; they will invent enough for themselves. It suffices to let them alone, to regard them with cheerful looks, and to check them if they get too excited. It is however good to make them feel, as far as is possible, the pleasures which the mind can give, such as conversation, news, stories and the various intellectual games which afford some instruction. All this will have its value at the proper time, but children's inclinations should never be forced in this direction. We should simply afford them the opportunities. One day their bodies will be less inclined to activity and then their minds will be all the more active.

The care which we take to give a zest to their serious occupations by means of pleasure will however contribute greatly to checking the eagerness of young people for dangerous amusements. It is subjection and boredom which make them so anxious to be amused. If a girl were less wearied with her mother's company she would be less inclined to get away from her in order to associate with undesirable companions.

In choosing amusements any doubtful society must be avoided. Girls must not associate with boys[17] or even with older girls whose conduct is not well-regulated and dependable. Games which make the child too wild or excited, or which involve bodily actions which are immodest for a girl, as well as frequent visits and conversations which may inspire a taste for paying calls, must be avoided. If one has not already been spoilt by amusement on a large scale and has not conceived some eager passion, one easily finds happiness; its true sources are good health and innocence. But those who have had the misfortune to become accustomed to violent pleasures lose the taste for moderate ones and are always wearying themselves in a restless search for happiness.

One spoils one's taste for amusements as for dishes. One can grow so accustomed to highly-seasoned food that if it is served in the ordinary way it becomes dull and insipid. Beware then of those emotional disturbances which result in weariness and disappointment. They are to be particularly dreaded in the case of children who have less power of resisting their feelings and who are ready always to give play to their emotions. Restrict them to a taste for simple things; there should be no extravagance either in the food which nourishes them or in the amusements which give them pleasure. Moderation always affords sufficient appetite without any need of stimulating it by seasonings which tend to excess. Temperance, says one of the ancients, is the best contriver of pleasure[18]—temperance which produces health of body and mind, and keeps one in a state of calm and restrained happiness. One has no need of artificial aids or shows or expense in order to procure enjoyment. Some little game which is invented, something read, a task undertaken, a walk, an artless conversation which refreshes after work, make one enjoy a more real happiness than the most alluring music.

Simple pleasures are, it is true, less vivid and lively. The other kind enrapture the soul by stimulating the passions to action. But simple pleasures have a better use. They afford just as much happiness, and this lasts without producing any ill effects. They are always beneficial, whereas the other kind of pleasure is like adulterated wines which at first give greater pleasure than pure ones, but which affect and harm the health. Not only the taste, but also the disposition of the soul, are vitiated by the search after these keen and intense pleasures. All that one can do for children who are in one's charge is to accustom them to a simple life, to strengthen them in this habit as long as one can, to warn them against the harm inherent in other pleasures, and never to leave them to themselves—as is usually done—at an age when the passions begin to make themselves felt and when, therefore, they most need to be kept in check.

It must be confessed that of all the difficulties in education none is comparable to that of bringing up children who are not responsive. Keen and responsive dispositions are certainly liable to dreadful aberrations; passion and pride seduce them; but at the same time there is great hope of them and they often return even though they have wandered far. Instruction is like a seed planted in them which grows and sometimes brings forth fruit when experience comes to the aid of reason and the passions cool down. In such cases one does at least know how it is possible to make children attentive and to arouse their curiosity. There is something in them which we can utilise to interest them in what we teach them and to put them on their mettle; whereas we have no lever on indolent natures. All their thoughts are wool-gathering; they are never where they ought to be. We cannot even make them really feel our correction. They hear everything and feel nothing. This indolence makes the child careless and gives him a distaste for everything he does. That is why the best education runs the risk of failing unless we take steps to circumvent this evil from the earliest childhood. Many people who are superficial conclude from their ill-success that nature is altogether responsible for making men of merit, and education not at all; whereas the truth is that there are some natures like barren land on which cultivation can do little. It is still worse when such education, difficult as it is, is thwarted or neglected or badly directed from the very first.

It should be noted that some children have dispositions about which we may be greatly deceived. At first they seem attractive because the early graces of childhood have a lustre which outshines everything else. They have a certain affectionateness and lovableness which prevents one examining their looks more closely. The mental gifts that we find in them surprise us because we do not expect these at that age. Any misjudgments which they make are pardoned and have the charm of ingenuousness. A certain activity of body, which never fails to show itself in children, is taken for activity of mind. The result is that childhood seems to promise so much and gives so little. A child who is conspicuous for his attainments at the age of five may grow less remarkable and less esteemed the older he gets. Of all the qualities which children possess there is only one on which you can count—and that is the power to reason well. It grows continually as they grow, if only it is well cultivated. Children's graces disappear, their liveliness vanishes, the warmth of their affections even is often lost because passions and intercourse with worldly people gradually harden young folk when they go out into society. Try then to discover beneath the grace of childhood whether the mind which you have to guide is lacking in natural curiosity and whether it is insensible to honourable emulation. If so, those who are concerned with the child's education can hardly avoid being repelled by so unprofitable and difficult a task. You should therefore lose no time in arousing the activities of the child's soul in order to awaken him from this sloth. If you can counteract this disadvantage you need not at first worry him with formal instruction. Beware of overloading his memory, for it is this that dulls and presses on the brain. Do not worry him with irksome rules; keep him cheerful. Since he may go to the other extreme of pride do not hesitate to show him with discretion of what he is capable. Be content with little; get him to notice the least improvement he makes. Show him how unfounded are his fears of not being able to succeed in the things which he can do quite well. Make use of emulation. Jealousy is stronger in children than is supposed. Sometimes they pine and waste away through a secret weakness because others are more loved or petted than they are. It is a cruelty only too common among mothers to make children suffer this torment; but one should know how to use this remedy against indolence when there is a pressing necessity. Put the child, whom you are bringing up, with other children who are doing a little better than he does. Examples disproportionate to his own weakness only serve to discourage him.

Allow him from time to time little triumphs over those of whom he is jealous. If you can, get him to laugh unaffectedly with you at his own timidity. Let him see other people who are just as timid as he is, but who succeed in getting the better of their disposition. Show him indirectly in conversation with someone else that timidity and lack of initiative stifle the spirit, that slack and indolent people, whatever their ability, become stupid and debase themselves. But beware of telling him these things in a stern and impatient voice, for nothing makes a child withdraw into himself more than does harshness. Rather redouble your attempts to make attractive the work which you cannot spare him, by rendering it as easy and pleasant as his nature allows. Sometimes it may even be necessary to spur him on by scorn and reproaches, but you should not do this yourself. Get some other inferior person—another child, for example—to do it without your seeming to know about this.

St Augustine tells how a rebuke administered to his mother, St Monica, in her childhood by a servant so affected her as to cure her of the bad habit of drinking wine unmixed—a habit from which the sternness and severity of her governess could not preserve her. Finally, an attempt should be made to inspire the minds of this type of child with a power of discrimination, just as one tries to inspire it in the bodies of certain invalids. We try to get them to seek after that which can overcome their distaste; we humour some of their fancies, even at the expense of what is prescribed, provided that they do not run to dangerous extremes. It is much more difficult to give this power of discrimination to those who have it not than to develop it in those in whom it as is yet not so fully formed as it should be.

There is another kind of feeling still more difficult and more important to inspire—the feeling of friendship. When the child is old enough it is no longer a question of turning his heart towards those who may be of use to him. Friendship will lead him to do almost anything that is demanded of him. This is a sure means of drawing him towards the good, if only one knows how to make use of it. All we need fear is excess or undesirable choice in his affections; but there are some children who are born artful and secretive, and who judge everything by their own interests. They deceive their parents who are blinded by their affection; they pretend to love them; they study their inclinations so as to conform to them; they appear more tractable than other children of the same age who act without concealment according as they feel; their cunning hides a stubborn will though this appears to be genuine meekness; and their deceitful disposition does not reveal itself fully until it is too late to remedy it.

If there is any childish disposition on which education can have no effect it can be said that this is it; and yet it must be confessed that the number of such children is much greater than is imagined. Parents cannot bring themselves to believe that their children are disposed towards evil. If they are not willing to see this for themselves no one dares to try to convince them of it, and so the evil continually grows. The best remedy would be to give children from their earliest years the fullest liberty to show their inclinations. We must always understand them thoroughly before we correct them. By nature they are simple and open; but if you obstruct them, however little, and set them an example of insincerity, they never return again to their original simplicity. It is true that God alone bestows affection and good nature. All we can do is to develop this by noble examples, by sentiments of honour and unselfishness, by disapproving of people who are too fond of themselves. We must try to make children, from their earliest years and before they have lost their natural unaffectedness, appreciate the pleasures of sincere and reciprocal friendship. Nothing will foster that better than putting them straightway in touch with people who never set them any example of harshness, insincerity, baseness or selfishness. It would be better to allow them to associate with people who have other faults, but are free from these. We should also praise children for anything which they do out of kindness, provided that it is not too much out of place or excessive. Parents too should show themselves full of sincere kindness towards their children; for the latter often learn from their parents themselves to love nothing. In short, I should like them never to be allowed to witness those empty compliments towards friends, those false shows of friendliness, and those artificial caresses by which they are encouraged to recompense with insincere formalities those whom they ought to love.

There is another fault, the reverse of that which I have just mentioned, which is very common in girls; it is to be passionately fond of quite ordinary things. They cannot see two people who are on bad terms without taking sides with one against the other. They are full of affection or aversion without any reason for it. They can see no faults in those whom they admire and no good qualities in those whom they despise. It is unwise at first to thwart them, for opposition will but strengthen these fancies; but one should gradually suggest to the young lady that one knows better than she all the good there is in those whom she loves and all the evil in those whom she dislikes. At the same time use any opportunity of making her see the failings of those who fascinate her and the good qualities possessed by those who displease her. Do not stress this. You will see that she will come to realise it for herself. After that, point out to her past infatuations and their most foolish manifestations. Say to her gently that she will find the same to be true of those of which she is not yet cured, when once they are over. Tell her of similar failings which you had at her age. Above all show her, as definitely as you can, the great mixture of good and evil that is found in everything that we can love or hate, so as to check the ardour of her likes and dislikes.

Never promise children ornaments or dainties as rewards. This has two evil effects—first it makes them value what they should despise; and secondly it deprives you of the means of employing other rewards which would aid your work. Be very careful not to threaten to make them study or to tie them down to some rule. You should have as few rules as possible, and when you cannot avoid making one it should be insinuated gently without giving it this name. You should always assign a reason for the suitability of doing something at one particular time and in one particular place, rather than in another.

One runs the risk of discouraging children if one never praises them when they do well. We see that St Paul often employs praise in order to encourage the weak and to insinuate correction the more gently. The Fathers have used the same method. It is true that to make praise useful it must be adapted so that it is free from exaggeration and flattery, and at the same time all the good must be referred to its true source—God. Children can also be rewarded by harmless games which contain something useful to do, by walks or by conversations which will not be without fruit, by little presents which serve as prizes—e.g. pictures, engravings, medals, geographical maps, books with gilt bindings.

CHAPTER VI

The use of history for children

Children are passionately fond of fairy-tales. At any time they can be seen in transports of joy or floods of tears when one tells them such stories. Do not fail to profit by this tendency. When you see that they are disposed to listen to you tell them some short and interesting fable;[19] but choose one about animals and let it be clever and harmless. Show the purpose of the fable and bring out the moral. As to heathen mythology, a girl will be fortunate if she knows nothing of these stories all her life long, because they are impure and full of absurd blasphemies. If you cannot prevent a child from hearing them inspire him with a horror of them. When you have told a child a fable wait till he asks you to tell him another; in this way leave him with a kind of hunger to hear more. Then, when his curiosity is excited, tell him some selected historical anecdotes, but in few words. Connect them together and postpone from day to day telling him the sequel so as to keep him in suspense and make him impatient to know the end. Enliven your stories by couching them in vivid and familiar language. Make your characters talk. Children whose imagination is lively will feel that they see and hear them. For example, tell the story of Joseph. Make his brothers speak brutally and Jacob like a loving and afflicted father. Make Joseph himself speak; let him take pleasure, when he is a ruler in Egypt, in hiding himself from his brothers so as to frighten them, and afterwards revealing himself to them. This homely presentation, together with the great interest of the story itself, will charm the child provided that you do not overload him with tales of this kind but let him long for them and even promise them as rewards if he is good. Never treat these stories as lessons and do not force the child to reproduce them. These reproductions, unless the child makes them spontaneously, weary him and take away all the pleasure from this kind of story.

None the less it should be noted that if the child has some aptitude for speaking he will of his own free will be disposed to recount to those whom he loves the stories which have given him the greatest pleasure. But do not make a rule of this. You can make use of someone who will be friendly with the child and who will seem to wish to hear his story. The child will be delighted to tell him. Pretend not to hear him. Let him tell it without correcting his mistakes. When he is more accustomed to telling stories you can explain to him gently the better way of doing this by making the story short, simple and direct, and by picking out the features which illustrate each point in the story. If you have several children accustom them gradually to act the characters in the stories which they have learnt. One will be Abraham, another Isaac. These dramas will appeal to the children more than other games and will accustom them to take pleasure in thinking and speaking about serious matters. They will fix these stories indelibly in their minds.

We should try to give them a greater liking for sacred stories than for other ones, not by telling them that these are more interesting—they probably will not believe that—but by making them feel this without saying so. Get them to realise how important they are, how unique, wonderful, true to life, full of splendid movement. The story of the creation, of Adam's fall, of the flood, of the call of Abraham, of the sacrifice of Isaac, of the adventures of Joseph to which I have already referred, of the birth and flight of Moses—these are calculated not merely to awaken a child's curiosity, but by revealing to him the origin of religion they lay its foundations in his mind. One is ignorant of the very basis of religion if one does not realise that it is altogether historical. It is from a series of wonderful events that we discover its establishment and its perpetuity, and all that we ought to do and believe. It should not be supposed that people have to be deeply versed in knowledge before they can appreciate these stories. They are short, varied and well-adapted to please the most uneducated. God who knows better than we do the spirit of man whom He has created, has put religion within the reach of everyone, so that far from overburdening the simple it may aid them to receive and retain its mysteries. For example, tell the child that in God there are three persons who are equal and have only one nature. By dint of hearing and repeating this phrase he will retain it in his memory; but I doubt whether he will understand its meaning. Tell him that when Jesus Christ went out of the water of Jordan the Father caused this voice from heaven to be heard: 'This is my beloved Son in Whom I am well pleased. Hear Him.' Go on to tell him that the Holy Spirit descended upon the Saviour in the form of a dove. You help the child to realise the Trinity clearly by means of a story which he will never forget. There are the three persons whom he will always distinguish by the difference of their actions; you will only have to teach him that together they are but one God. This example is sufficient to show the value of stories. Although they seem to prolong instructions, in reality they shorten it greatly and they avoid the dullness of catechisms in which dogmas are dissociated from events. We can see that in ancient times instruction was given by means of stories. The admirable method by which St Augustine advises us to instruct the ignorant was not one which this Father alone introduced; it was the universal method and practice of the Church. It consisted in showing by the progress of history that religion is as old as the world—Jesus Christ expected in the Old Testament and Jesus Christ reigning in the New. This is the basis of Christian instruction.

This requires a little more time and trouble than the instruction to which most people confine themselves; but when one knows these details one knows religion thoroughly, whereas when one is ignorant of them one has only confused ideas about Jesus Christ, the gospel, the Church, the necessity of submitting unreservedly to its decisions, and the stock of virtues which the name of Christian should inspire in us. The recently published *Historical Catechism*[20] is a short and simple book, much clearer than the ordinary catechisms, and it contains everything that should be known on this subject, so that it cannot be said that much study is needed. Its aim is indeed that also of the Council of Trent, with the difference that in the Council's Catechism there are rather too many theological terms for ordinary people.

Add to the stories which I have mentioned the crossing of the Red Sea, the sojourn of the people of Israel in the desert where they ate bread which came down from heaven and drank water which Moses caused to flow from a rock by striking it with his rod. Describe the miraculous conquest of the Promised Land when the waters of Jordan flowed towards their source and the walls of a city fell down of their own accord at the sight of the besiegers. Picture vividly the battles of Saul and David. Show the latter in his youth, unarmed and in a shepherd's dress, conqueror of the proud giant Goliath. Do not omit the glory and wisdom of Solomon. Make him decide between the two women who disputed for a child; but show him falling from his high estate of wisdom and bringing dishonour on himself by self-indulgence—the almost inevitable result of too great prosperity.

Let them hear the prophets speaking to kings in the name of God. Show how they were able to read the future like a book, how they were humble, self-denying, enduring continual persecution for having spoken the truth. Then go on to describe the first fall of Jerusalem. Show the Temple in flames and the Holy City in ruins owing to the sins of the people. Tell of the captivity in Babylon where the Jews bewailed their beloved Sion. Before the return tell them the delightful stories of Tobit and Judith, of Esther and Daniel. It would even be of advantage to discuss with children the different characters of these holy persons, so as to decide which they liked best. One would prefer Esther, another Judith; and that would stimulate among them a little discussion which would impress these stories more deeply in their memories and form their judgments. Then restore the Chosen People to Jerusalem and make them rebuild its ruins; describe in glowing colours their peace and happiness. Soon after draw a portrait of the cruel and impious Antiochus who died in insincere penitence. Show the victories of the Maccabees in this persecutor's reign, and the martyrdom of the seven brothers of this name. Come on to the miraculous birth of St John. Describe in greater detail that of Jesus Christ. Then you should select from the Gospels the most striking events of His life: His preaching in the Temple at the age of twelve; His baptism and retirement into the desert and temptation; the calling of the apostles; the miracle of the loaves; the conversion of the woman who was a sinner and who anointed the Saviour's feet with ointment, washed them with her tears, and wiped them with her hair. Picture the Samaritan woman, the man born blind who was healed, Lazarus raised to life, Our Lord's triumphant entry into Jerusalem. Let them witness His passion; describe Him rising from the tomb. Stress the familiar intercourse which He had with His disciples during the great forty days, until they saw Him ascend into heaven.

Describe the descent of the Holy Ghost, the stoning of St Stephen, the conversion of St Paul, the calling of the centurion Cornelius. The journeys of the apostles, and particularly those of St Paul, are also very interesting. Select the most wonderful stories of the martyrs and outline the heavenly life of the early Christians. Do not overlook the courage of young virgins, the amazing austerities of the solitaries, the conversion of emperors and of the Empire, the blindness of the Jews and their terrible punishment[21] which still endures.

All these stories, if properly handled, will pleasantly fill the imagination of young and intelligent children with the history of religion from the creation of the world down to our own times and will give them an exalted idea of it which will never fade. They will even see in this story the hand of God always ready to save the just and to confound the unjust. They will grow accustomed to seeing God always and everywhere at work, surely bending to His will those of His creatures who seem furthest removed from Him. But we should select from these stories whatever produces the most attractive and impressive effect because we must make use of every means to render religion beautiful, alluring and dignified, and not something wearisome and dull—as is usually done.

In addition to the priceless advantage of teaching children religion in this way, this collection of pleasant stories, which are committed to memory while they are still young, rouses their curiosity with regard to serious subjects, renders them susceptible to intellectual pleasures, and makes them interested in other stories which they hear told and which have some connection with those that they already know. But, once again, be very careful to avoid forcing them to listen or to remember these stories, and still less make them a regular lesson. Pleasure must do everything. Do not press them. You will succeed even with children of moderate ability. You have only to avoid overloading them, and to let their curiosity develop gradually. But, you will say, how does one tell them stories in a lively, succinct, natural and pleasant fashion? Where are the governesses[22] who know how to do that? To this I reply that all I propose is that persons of good intellectual equipment should be chosen to look after children and that they should be encouraged, as far as possible, to use this method of instruction. Each governess will employ it as far as she can. But however little aptitude she has for intellectual things the attempt will be less unsuccessful if she adopts this natural and simple method.

We can always supplement our stories by showing engravings or pictures which attractively illustrate Bible history. Engravings serve very well and ordinarily these should be employed. But if one has the opportunity to show children good pictures it must not be neglected, for their imagination is struck much more forcibly by the appeal of colour and the fact that the figures are life-like.

CHAPTER VII

How to give children their first ideas of religion

We have already pointed out that children are not able to reason in their earliest years. This is not to say that they have not already the idea and general principles of reason which will develop later; but because they lack knowledge of many facts they cannot apply their reason, and in addition the instability of their minds prevents them from following out their thoughts and linking them together.

It is none the less necessary, without pressing them, to turn their earliest attempts at reason towards a knowledge of God. Persuade them of the truths of Christianity without giving them occasion to doubt. They hear of someone's death; they know that he is being buried. Say to the child: 'Is the dead man in the grave?' 'Yes.' 'Is he not in heaven?' 'I am sorry. Yes, he is.' 'How then can he be in the grave and in heaven at the same time?' 'It is his soul that is in heaven and his body that has been buried in the earth.' 'His soul then is not the same as his body?' 'No.' 'His soul is not dead?' 'No, it will live for ever in heaven.' Go on to say: 'And you—do you want to be saved?' 'Yes.' 'But what does being saved mean?' 'That one's soul goes to heaven when one dies.' 'And what is death?' 'It is when the soul leaves the body and the body returns to its dust.'

I do not suggest that we should expect our children at first to answer like this, though I can none the less affirm that several have made me these answers from the age of four. But I have in mind a less open and developed nature. The next best thing is to wait patiently for a year or two.

You should show the child a house and get him to realise that it was not built of itself. The stones, you will say to him, were not put in position without someone to carry them. It is even advisable to show him the masons at work. Then make him look at the heavens, the earth, the chief things that God has made for the use of man. Say to him: See how much more beautiful and better made the world is than a house. Was it made of itself? No; surely not. It is God who made it with His own hands.

At first follow the method of Scripture. Strike the child's imagination. Never put anything to him unless it is expressed in concrete form. Show God seated on a throne, with eyes more brilliant than the rays of the sun and more piercing than lightning. Make Him speak. Give Him ears which hear everything, hands which sustain the universe, arms always ready to punish the wicked, a tender and fatherly heart to render happy those who love Him. The time will come when you will render all these ideas more definite. Watch for any opportunity which the child's mind offers you; try in various ways to discover how best the great truths may find access to his brain. Above all never tell him anything new without making it clear to him by some concrete comparison.

For example, ask him if he would rather die than deny Jesus Christ. He will answer: 'Yes'. Go on to say: 'What, would you let your head be cut off in order to get to heaven?' 'Yes.' So far the child thinks that he would have sufficient courage to do it; but you, who want him to realise that he can do nothing without grace, will not gain anything if you simply say that one needs grace in order to be faithful. He will not understand an expression like that, and if you accustom him to use it without understanding it you have made no progress. What then is to be done? Tell him the story of St Peter. Show him how he said in a proud voice: 'Though I should die with Thee, I will follow Thee. If all the rest leave Thee I will never forsake Thee.' Then describe his fall. He denies Jesus Christ three times; a maid-servant makes him afraid. Tell the child why God allowed him to be so weak. Then compare him with a child or a sick person who cannot walk alone; and make him understand that we have need of God to carry us as a nurse carries a child. In this way you will make him appreciate the mystery of grace.[23]

But the most difficult truth to explain is that we have souls which are more precious than our bodies. We accustom children from their early years to talk about their souls; and we do well, for although they do not understand they do get a confused idea of the difference between soul and body until the time comes when they are able to realise it. Just as childish misconceptions are fatal when they lead to error, so they are useful when they inure the imagination to truth until such time as the reason may be able to deal with it by argument. But we must ensure real conviction. How can that be done? Is it by plunging a girl into the subtleties of philosophy? Nothing is so bad. We must confine ourselves to making clear and intelligible to her, as far as is possible, that which she is continually hearing and talking about.

As to her body, she already knows too much about that. Everything encourages her to humour it, to adorn it, to make an idol of it. It is of first importance to inspire her with a contempt for it by showing her something better in herself.

Say to a child whose reason has already begun to develop: 'Is it your soul that eats?' If he gives the wrong answer do not scold him, but tell him gently that the soul does not eat; it is the body, you will say, that eats; it is the body that is like the beasts. 'Have beasts souls? Have they intellects?' The child will answer: 'No.' 'But they eat,' you will continue, 'even though they have no souls. You can see clearly therefore that it is not the soul that eats. It is the body which takes food for nourishment; it is the body that walks and sleeps. And what does the soul do? It reasons, it has knowledge of the world, it likes certain things and regards others with aversion.' Add, in a joking way: 'You see this table?' 'Yes.' 'You recognise it then?' 'Yes.' 'You can see plainly that it is not made like this chair; you know perfectly well that it is made of wood and not like the chimney-piece which is of stone?' 'Yes', will be the child's answer. Do not proceed until you realise from the tone of his voice and the expression of his eyes that these simple truths have struck him. Then say: 'But does the table know you?' You will see that the child begins to laugh at the absurdity of this question. Never mind. Go on to say: 'Which loves you best—this table or this chair?' He will laugh again. Continue: 'And is this window well-behaved?' Then go a step further: 'Does this doll reply when you speak to it?' 'No.' 'Why? Has it no soul?' 'No, it has not.' 'It is not like you then, for you know it but it does not know you. But after your death, when you are under the ground, won't you be like this doll?' 'Yes.' 'You will have no more feelings?' 'No.' 'And your soul will be in heaven?' 'Yes.' 'Will it not see God there?' 'Yes, that is true.' 'And as for the doll's soul where is it now?' You will see the child smiling as he tells you, or at any rate makes you understand, that the doll has no soul.

On this basis and by little devices employed from time to time you can accustom the child to ascribe to the body what belongs to it and to the soul that which comes from it, provided that you do not inadvertently suggest to him certain actions which are common to both alike. You must avoid subtleties which might obscure these truths and content yourself with distinguishing clearly the things in which the difference between body and soul is most definitely marked. It is possible to find minds so unintelligent that even with a good education they cannot comprehend these truths clearly. However, not only does one sometimes understand a thing pretty well even though one cannot explain it thoroughly, but also God sees in the minds of men better than we what He has put there for the comprehension of His mysteries.

As for children in whom you see an intelligence capable of going further you can, without committing them to a course of study which seems too much like philosophy, make them realise—as far as their capacity allows—what they mean when they are made to say that God is a spirit, and that their soul is a spirit also. I think that the best and simplest way of making them understand the spiritual nature of God and the soul is to show them the difference between a dead man and a living one. In the former there is only a body; in the latter the body is united with the spirit. Then make them see that what can reason[24] is much more complete than what has only shape and movement. Then make them realise by some examples that bodies do not perish, but merely break up. Thus the substance of wood which is burnt turns into ashes or is given off in the form of smoke. If therefore—you will add—what is in itself but ash, incapable of knowledge or thought, never perishes how much more will our souls, which can both know and think, never cease to exist? The body may die—i.e. it may be separated from the soul and become ashes—but the soul will live, for it will always be capable of thought.

Those who teach should develop to the full these thoughts in the child's mind, for they are the basis of all religion. But when they cannot achieve this, instead of being disheartened by stubborn and backward natures, they should hope that God will secretly enlighten them. There is indeed a clear and practical way of strengthening the realisation of the difference between body and soul. It is to accustom children to despise the one and honour the other in every detail of conduct. Praise instruction which nourishes and develops the soul; honour the noble truths which inspire it to become wise and good. Condemn luxury, finery and everything which weakens the body; make children realise how far honour, good conscience and religion are above carnal pleasures. By such sentiments and without any reasoning about soul and body the ancient Romans taught their children to despise their bodies and to sacrifice them in order to give the soul the pleasure of achieving virtue and glory. With them it was not merely persons of high rank, but the whole people, who were by nature temperate, unselfish, full of contempt for life, keenly susceptible to honour and wisdom. When I speak of the ancient Romans I mean those who lived before the growth of their empire which changed the simplicity of their manners.

It should not be said that it would be impossible to instil such principles as these in children by means of education. How many practices do we see established among us contrary to reason but by the force of custom! For example, that of duelling[25] which is founded upon a false code of honour. It was not by reasoning, but by taking for granted without reason this practice based on the code of honour, that one risked one's life, and every man who wore a sword lived in constant danger. A man who had no quarrel could at any time be exposed to one with people who were looking for pretexts to distinguish themselves in some fight. However restrained one was one could not, without losing false honour, either avoid a quarrel by giving an explanation or refuse to encounter the first comer who wanted to fight. What authority has been necessary in order to eradicate so barbarous a custom! See then how powerful are the influences of education. They will be even more powerful in engendering virtue if they are upheld by reason and the hopes of heaven hereafter. The Romans, of whom we have spoken already, and before them the Greeks, in the heyday of their republics brought up their children to despise luxury and effeminacy. They taught them to value glory alone and to desire, not to possess riches, but to vanquish the kings who possessed them and to believe that happiness was attainable only through virtue. This spirit was so firmly established in these republics that, in virtue of these principles, so different from those of other peoples, they performed incredible deeds. The example of many martyrs and other early Christians of all conditions and ages shows that the grace of baptism, aided by education, can produce even more wonderful effects on the faithful by making them despise what belongs to the body. Seek then all the most pleasing devices and most striking comparisons in order to show children that in our bodies we are like to the beasts, but in our souls to the angels. Tell them that the soul is to the body like a rider who manages his horse. End by saying that the soul is very weak and unhappy if it allows itself to be carried away by its body, like a fiery steed which throws its rider down a precipice. Point out also that the beauty of the body is as a flower which opens in the morning, but in the evening fades and is trampled underfoot; whereas the soul is the image of the immortal beauty of God. You should add that there is an order of things so much the more excellent that they cannot be seen by the eyes of the flesh, since everything seen here below is subject to change and corruption. In order to make children realise that there are very real things which our eyes and ears cannot perceive we must ask them whether it is not true that one person is wise and another has plenty of intelligence. When they reply:

'Yes', go on to say: 'But have you seen so-and-so's wisdom? What colour is it? Have you heard it? Does it make much noise? Have you touched it? Is it cold or hot?' The child will laugh and he will do the same at similar questions about the intelligence. He will appear astonished that anyone should ask him what colour an intelligence is, or whether it is round or square. Thus you will be able to make him realise that there are some very real things which can neither be seen nor touched nor heard, and that these things are spiritual. But in the case of girls you must enter upon this kind of conversation tactfully. I suggest this only in the case of those whose curiosity and powers of reasoning encourage you to put these questions. You must regulate yourself according to the capacity of their understanding and their needs.

As far as possible keep their understanding within ordinary limits and teach them that their sex should show a restraint as regards learning almost as delicate as that which inspires a horror of vice. At the same time the imagination should be made to come to the assistance of the understanding in order to give them attractive images, which the body cannot see, of the truths of religion. You must describe the glory of heaven as St John pictures it: all tears wiped away; no more death, no pain or weeping; sighing will flee away, evils will vanish; an eternal bliss will rest upon the heads of the blessed as the waters upon the head of a man sunk to the bottom of the sea. Show them the glorious Jerusalem of which God Himself will be the sun to produce an unending day; a river of peace, a stream of joys, a fountain of life will water it; all will be of gold and pearls and precious stones. I am well aware that all these images apply to earthly things, but after having gained children's attention by such an attractive picture you can make use of the means which I have already described to bring them back to spiritual things.

End by saying that we are here like travellers at an inn or in a tent; that the body will perish; that it cannot be kept from corruption for more than a few years, but that the soul will fly away to that heavenly country where it will live for ever with God. If one can help children to get the habit of contemplating these great truths with pleasure and estimating everyday things by comparison with such lofty hopes, we shall smooth out innumerable difficulties.

I would like also to try to impress strongly upon them the fact of the resurrection of the body. Teach them that Nature is only a system established by God in His works, and miracles are merely exceptions from these general rules. Thus it is no more for God to perform a hundred miracles than for me to leave my room a quarter of an hour before the usual time. Next recall the story of the resurrection of Lazarus and that of Jesus Christ and of His appearances during forty days to so many persons. Finally show them that it would not be difficult for Him who created men to re-create them. Do not forget the comparison with the grain of wheat which is sown in the ground and which rots there, that it may be raised again and multiplied.

After all, it is not a question of making children learn morality by heart, as if it were a catechism. This method only results in turning religion into meaningless language, or at any rate into tedious formalities. Confine yourself to helping them to understand it, and put them in the way of discovering these truths for themselves. These will thus make the greater impression. Profit by opportunities to enable them to see more clearly what at present they see only indistinctly.

But notice carefully that there is nothing so dangerous as to speak to children about despising this present life unless you make them realise, by the whole course of your behaviour, that you are speaking in serious earnest. At any age example exerts an astonishing influence upon us. In childhood it is all-powerful. Children delight to imitate and they have not as yet habits which make the imitation of someone else difficult. Moreover, as they are not able of themselves to judge the reasons for things, they judge of them more by what they see in those who put them forward than by the reasons on which they depend. Actions speak louder than words. If therefore children see done the opposite of what is taught to them they become accustomed to regard religion as a fine ceremony and virtue as an impracticable abstraction.

Never in front of children make fun of matters relating to religion. One may ridicule the devotions of some simple soul, or laugh at what he wishes to ask his confessor or at the penances which are imposed upon him. You may think that there is no harm in all this, but you are wrong. In such matters everything is important. We should never speak about God or things concerning religion but with a seriousness and reverence far removed from these liberties. Often people who are most circumspect about worldly proprieties are the most indecorous about religious ones.

When the child has thought sufficiently to have knowledge of himself and of God, associate with this the facts of history which he has already learned. He will see with pleasure the connection between his own reflections and the history of the human race. He will have recognised that man is not made for himself, but that his soul is the image of God and his body has been formed from so many wonderful elements by a divine industry and power—and this will put him in mind of the story of the creation. Then he will consider that man was born with propensities contrary to reason, that he is led astray by pleasure, carried away by anger, and that his body drags his soul after it, in spite of reason, just as a spirited horse runs away with its rider; whereas the soul ought to control the body. He will perceive the cause of this evil in the history of Adam's fall; and this history too will make him look to the Saviour who is to reconcile men to God. There is the whole basis of religion.

In order to enable young people to understand better the mysteries, acts and teaching of Jesus Christ they must be encouraged to read the Gospels. They should be prepared betimes to read the word of God, just as they are prepared to receive the body of Jesus Christ in the Eucharist.[26] The fundamental principle to be laid down is the authority of the Church, the spouse of the Son of God and the mother of all the faithful. We must listen to her, you will say, because the Holy Spirit enlightens her so that she may explain the Scriptures to us. We can come to Jesus Christ only by means of her. Never fail to read to children those passages where Jesus Christ promises to uphold and vivify the Church in order that she may lead her children in the way of truth. Above all inspire girls with that wise restraint which St Paul recommends. Help them to beware of the snare of novelty, the love of which is so characteristic of their sex. Arm them with a salutary dread of any singularity in religious matters. Set before them that heavenly perfection, that wonderful discipline, which was found among the early Christians. Help them to be ashamed of our present-day laxity and to aim at evangelical purity; but at the same time to be very careful to guard against all presumptuously critical thoughts and indiscreet reforms.

Aim then at setting before them the Gospel and the great examples of olden times, but do so only after having tested their receptivity and the simplicity of their faith. Relate everything to the Church. Show how, with the promises which were made to her and the authority which she is given in the Gospel, during all the passing of the centuries and in spite of so many attacks and revolutions, she has preserved the apostolic succession and the faith, which are the obvious fulfilment of the divine promises. If only you lay the foundation of humility, of submission, and of rejection of any heretical singularity, you will very successfully show young people all that is most perfect in the law of God, in the institution of the sacraments, and in the practice of the primitive Church. I know that one cannot give this instruction in all its fullness to all kinds of children; I merely suggest that it should be given as definitely as is possible, according to the opportunities afforded and the disposition of the minds with which we have to deal.

In the case of the female sex superstition[27] is doubtless to be feared, but nothing eradicates it or prevents it better than solid instruction. This—although it must be kept within proper limits and far removed from the studies of the learned—can none the less go much further than is commonly believed. Some people think they are well educated who are not so at all. Their ignorance is so great that they cannot realise how far they are from understanding the principles of Christianity. Nothing, which cannot be derived from the Gospel or authorised by the consistent approval of the Church, must ever be allowed to become mixed up with the Faith or with religious practices. We must tactfully warn children against certain abuses which are so common that one might almost regard them as characteristics of the discipline of the Church, unless one were otherwise instructed. We can guard against them only by going back to the fountain-head, by knowing the origin of these things, and the practice of the saints themselves.

For this reason accustom girls, who are by nature credulous, not to accept too readily certain stories which are without foundation, not to be too much given to certain devotions introduced by indiscreet enthusiasm without waiting until the Church approves them. The real means of teaching them what one should think about these matters is not to criticise practices which have often been introduced by pious motives, but to show, without censuring them, that they are devoid of a solid foundation. Be content never to introduce these matters in the instruction which you give them about Christianity. This silence will suffice to accustom children from the beginning to form a concept of Christianity in all its completeness and perfection, without adding these practices. Later you can prepare them easily to withstand the arguments of the Calvinists. I think that such instructions will be quite useful because every day we have to mix with people who hold their views and talk about them in ordinary conversation.

They charge us, you will say, with unwarranted concern about images, the invocation of the saints, prayers for the dead, indulgences. See what they make of the Church's teaching on baptism, confirmation, the sacrifice of the Mass, penitence, confession, the authority of the clergy, among whom the Pope is the chief by the institution of Jesus Christ Himself, and of the Holy See from which we cannot be separated without leaving the

Church. There, you will add, is the sum of our belief. What the Calvinists accuse us of adding is not Catholic doctrine, but it raises an obstacle to their reunion if they are required to submit themselves to opinions which offend them and which the Church disavows; as if these opinions were part of our faith. At the same time never fail to show how often the Calvinists rashly condemn the most ancient and sacred ceremonies; but add that practices more recently instituted, if they are in harmony with the ancient spirit, deserve a profound respect because the authority which establishes them is always the immortal spouse of the Son of God.

In speaking to them thus of those who have stolen away part of their flock from their original pastors, under pretext of reformation, do not fail to point out how these proud men have overlooked human weakness and made it impossible for the humble to practise religion, since they wish individuals to judge for themselves in the Scriptures all the articles of the Christian faith, without submitting to the interpretation given by the Church. Show them that among the faithful Holy Scripture is the sovereign rule of belief. We recognise, you will say, no less than the heretics that the Church must be guided by the Scriptures, but we claim that the Holy Spirit aids the Church in interpreting them properly. It is not that we prefer the Church to the Scriptures, but rather the interpretation of the Scriptures made by the universal Church to our own private interpretation. Is it not the height of pride and temerity for an individual to suspect that the Church is mistaken in its interpretation, and not to be afraid of being deceived by making a decision contrary to hers?

Encourage children to wish to know the reasons for all the ceremonies and expressions used in the divine office and the administration of the sacraments. Show them the font and let them see a baptism. Let them note how on Holy Thursday the sacred oils are consecrated and how on the Saturday the water in the font is blessed. Give them a taste for sermons—not those which are full of affectation and show, but those which are sensible and edifying, like the homilies which help them to understand clearly the essence of the Gospel. Call their attention to what is noble and touching in the simplicity of this teaching, and inspire in them a love of their parish church where the pastor speaks with unction and with authority, however little talent he possesses. At the same time make them admire and respect those communities which co-operate in the service of the Church. Never let them make fun of the religious life or habit. Stress the holiness of the religious orders and the benefit which religion derives from them, and the enormous number of Christian people who attain in these holy retreats a perfection which is almost impossible amid the distractions of the world. Let children be accustomed to hear death spoken of, to see, without being troubled, a funeral pall, an open tomb, invalids on their death-beds, and dead bodies—if you can do so without exposing them to a shock of fear.

There is nothing more disturbing than to see so many persons of intelligence and piety unable to think of death without shuddering. Others will turn pale if they find that they are thirteen at table or because they have had a certain kind of dream or have seen salt spilt. The fear of all these imaginary omens is a relic of sheer paganism. Although women have not the same opportunities as men to show their courage they still ought to possess it. Cowardice is always despicable and everywhere has evil effects. A woman ought to know how to face false alarms and be firm against unforeseen dangers. She should never weep or be afraid unless there is serious justification; she should be upheld by force of character. When one is a Christian—of either sex—it is not permissible to be a coward. The essence of Christianity, if one may say so, is contempt of this present life and love of the life hereafter.

CHAPTER VIII

Instruction on the ten commandments, the sacraments and prayer

The most important image to set before the eyes of children is that of Jesus Christ, the author and finisher of our faith, the centre of all religion and our only hope. I do not undertake here to say how we should teach the mystery of the incarnation, for this would take me too far and there are plenty of books in which everything necessary to be taught should be regulated by the example of Jesus Christ Himself, Who assumed a mortal body in order to teach us how to live and die, by showing us in His own flesh, similar to our own, all that we ought to believe and practise. This does not mean that at every moment we should be comparing the child's thoughts and actions with the life of Jesus Christ; such a comparison would become tedious and ill-judged. But children should be accustomed to look upon the life of Christ as our example and His words as our law. Select among His teachings and His acts those which are within the child's grasp. If he complains of suffering some inconvenience, remind him of Jesus Christ on the cross. If he cannot reconcile himself to some disagreeable task, show him Jesus Christ working till the age of thirty in a carpenter's shop. If he wishes to be praised and honoured tell him of the insults which were heaped upon the Saviour. If he cannot put up with the people with whom he comes into contact let him see Jesus Christ associating with the most abandoned sinners and hypocrites. If he shows some resentment hasten to show him Jesus Christ dying on the cross even for those who were putting Him to death. If he gives way to immoderate joy describe to him the gentleness and modesty of Jesus Christ Whose whole life was calm and restrained. In short, get him to imagine what Jesus Christ would think and say about our conversations and amusements and our most serious occupations if He were still among us. What would be our astonishment, you will go on to say, if He were suddenly to appear in the midst of us when we were totally forgetful of His law! But is it not this that will happen to each one of us in the hour of death and to the whole world at the day of judgment? Therefore we must describe the break-down of the mechanism of the universe—the sun darkened, the stars falling from their places, the elements in flames and flowing like rivers of fire, the very foundations of the earth shaken. How then should we regard this heaven which covers us, this earth which supports us, these dwellings in which we live, all the familiar objects which surround us, seeing that they are destined to be burnt up? Go on to describe the open tombs, the dead re-formed from the remains of their bodies, Jesus Christ descending in majesty from the clouds, the open book in which will be written the inmost secrets of our hearts, the sentence pronounced in the face of all nations and generations, the glory of an unfading crown which will be proclaimed for the just who will reign together with Jesus Christ, and finally the lake of fire and brimstone, the night of everlasting horror, the gnashing of teeth, the agony shared with the demons, which will be the fate of the souls of sinners.

Do not fail to explain thoroughly the Ten Commandments. Make clear that they are a summary of the law of God and that in the Gospel one can find indirectly what is contained in the Decalogue. Make clear what is meant by a piece of advice, and guard the children whom you are teaching against deluding themselves—as so many people do—by pushing too far the distinction between advice and precept. Point out that advice is given to make precepts more easy, to strengthen men against their own frailty, to draw them back from the edge of the precipice to which they are carried by their own weight; and in short that advice becomes a definite precept for those who, in certain circumstances, cannot observe precepts without advice. For example, people who are too susceptible to the love of this world and the snares of human society are obliged to follow the evangelical advice to quit everything and retire into a solitude. Often repeat that the letter killeth, but the spirit giveth life; that is to say, simply observing the outward forms of worship is useless and harmful if it is not inwardly illuminated by the spirit of love and religion. Make this quite clear. Show that God wishes to be honoured with the heart and not with the lips, that ceremonies serve to express and to stimulate our religion, but that ceremonies are not religion itself, because this is something inward and God seeks worshippers in spirit and in truth; that we must love Him in our hearts and consider ourselves as if in all nature there was but God and ourselves. He has no need of our words and our acts of adoration, nor even of our wealth. What He wants is ourselves. We ought not to carry out merely what the law ordains, but should try to fulfil it with the aim of achieving what it had in view when it was formulated. Thus it is nothing to hear Mass if one does not do so in order to unite oneself to Jesus Christ Who was sacrificed for us, and to edify oneself by everything which His sacrifice represents. End by saying that those who cry 'Lord, Lord' will not enter into the Kingdom of Heaven, and that if one does not achieve the true realisation of the love of God, renunciation of temporal things, contempt of oneself and detestation of the world, one makes Christianity a misleading mirage both for oneself and for everyone else.

Let us go on to consider the sacraments. I presume that you have already explained their ceremonies so far as they have been performed in the child's presence—as I have said before. This is the best way of making him realise their spirit and purpose. By this means you can make him understand how great a thing it is to be a Christian and how shameful and fatal it is to be worldly. Recall often the exorcisms[28] and promises which are made in the ceremony of baptism in order to show that the examples and maxims of the world, so far from having any authority over us, ought to make us distrust everything that comes from so hateful and poisonous a source. Do not shrink even from picturing—as St Paul does—the devil reigning in the world and exciting the hearts of men by the violent passions which lead them to seek riches and glory and pleasure. This pomp, you will say, is even more that of the devil than of the world. This is a spectacle of vanity to which no Christian should open either his eyes or his heart. The first step that one takes in Christian baptism is to renounce all worldly pomp. To go back to the world after having made such solemn promises to God is to fall into a kind of apostasy, like a religious who, in spite of his vows, leaves his cloister and his penitential garb in order to go back into the world.

Add that we should trample underfoot the ill-judged scorn, the irreverent mocking and even assaults of the world since confirmation makes us soldiers of Jesus Christ in order to fight this enemy. The bishop, you will say, struck[29] you in order to inure you against the hardest blows of persecution. He anointed you with holy oil in order to imitate the men of old who anointed themselves in order to make their bodies more supple and vigorous when they went out to fight. Finally he signed you with the cross to show that you must be crucified with Jesus Christ. We are no longer, you will continue, in the time of persecutions when those who refuse to deny the Gospel are put to death; but the world which can never cease to be the world—i.e. corrupt—is always indirectly persecuting the faithful. It sets snares to secure their downfall, it vilifies them and makes fun of them. It makes the practice of piety so difficult under most conditions that even in the heart of Christian nations, where the sovereign authority supports Christianity, one is in danger of being ashamed of the name of Jesus Christ and of following His example.

Stress strongly the happiness which we have by being incorporated with Jesus Christ in the Eucharist. In baptism He makes us His brethren; in the Eucharist He makes us His members. Just as by His incarnation He took upon Him our general human nature, so by the Eucharist (which is a quite natural continuation of the incarnation) He gives Himself to each individual believer. Everything is real in these mysteries. Jesus Christ gives His flesh as truly as He took it at His incarnation; but to eat the life-giving flesh of Jesus Christ without living according to His spirit is to render oneself guilty of the

Lord's body and blood and to eat and drink damnation. He Himself says 'He who eats my flesh must live for me'.

But what a misfortune, you will go on to say, it is to have need of the sacrament of penance which implies that one has sinned after one has been made a child of God. This heavenly power, which is exercised on earth and which God has put into the hands of His priests to remit or retain sins as may be necessary, is a wonderful source of mercy; but we should none the less tremble with fear of abusing the gifts and patience of God. As the body of Jesus Christ is the life, the strength and the consolation of the just, it is to be earnestly desired that one can feed upon it every day; but for the remedy of sick souls it is to be hoped that they may attain such a state of health that day by day they have less need of it. Whatever one does the need will be only too great; but it would be much worse if during the whole of one's life one should go through a constant scandalous round of sinning and repenting. The only purpose of confession, then, is conversion and self-correction; otherwise the words of absolution, however powerful they may be according to Christ's institution, remain mere words owing to our indifference. But they are also words of ill omen which might be our condemnation before God. A confession without inward change, so far from relieving the conscience from the burden of sin, only adds a dreadful sacrilege to the other sins.

Have the prayers for the dying[30] read to the children whom you are educating. They are admirable. Show what the Church does and says in administering extreme unction, and what a consolation it is to the dying to receive a renewal of the sacred unction for their last combat. But to be worthy of these favours in time of death one must have been faithful to those granted during life.

Admire the riches of the grace of Christ Who did not disdain to apply the remedy to the very origin of evil by sanctifying the source of our birth, which is marriage. How appropriate it was to make a sacrament of this union between a man and a woman which represents that of the Creator with his creature and of Jesus Christ with His Church. This benediction was necessary in order to moderate the carnal affections of men, to shed abroad peace and consolation over all families, and to hand on religion as an inheritance from one generation to another. From this we can conclude that marriage is a most holy and pure estate, though less perfect than virginity, that one should be called to it, that one should not seek it for the sake of gross pleasures or worldly pomp, but it should be desired only for the formation of saints.

Praise the infinite wisdom of the Son of God Who has ordained pastors to be His representatives among us, to instruct us in His name, to give us His body, to reconcile us to Him after our falling away, to form every day new believers and even new pastors who will lead us when they themselves are gone, so that the Church may be preserved throughout the ages without interruption. Explain how glad we should be that God has given such power to men, and with what religious feeling we should regard the anointed of the Lord. They are men of God and dispensers of His mysteries. We should therefore withdraw our eyes and lament if we see in them the least blemish which tarnishes the lustre of their ministry. It could be wished indeed that we could wash it away with our own blood. Their doctrine is not their own. Whosoever hears them hears Jesus Christ Himself. When they are met in the name of Jesus Christ to explain the Scriptures the Holy Spirit speaks together with them. Their time is not at their own disposal, and they ought not therefore to be expected to descend from so high a ministry, in which they should devote themselves to preaching and to prayer, in order to act as mediators between God and man or to stoop to worldly affairs. Still less should they wish to make profit from their revenues which are the patrimony of the poor. But the worst abuse of all is to try to raise one's relations or friends[31] to this most honourable ministry for purposes of temporal advantage.

It remains to demonstrate the necessity for prayer, founded on the need for grace, as I have already explained. God, you will tell the child, wills that we should pray to Him for this grace, not because He is ignorant of our needs, but because He wishes to accustom us to a habit of prayer which makes us conscious of our needs. Thus what He requires of us is the humiliation of our hearts, the realisation of our misery and feebleness, and our confidence in His goodness. These prayers which He demands of us consist only in our intention and our desire, for He has no need of words. Often one repeats many words without really praying, and one often prays inwardly without saying a single word. Yet words may be very useful for they excite in us the thoughts and feelings which they express, if we pay attention to them. It is for this reason that Jesus Christ has given us a form of prayer. What a consolation it is to know from Jesus Christ Himself how His Father wills us to pray! What power there should be in the petitions which God Himself puts into our mouths. Surely He will grant us that which He has taken care to teach us to ask! After this, explain how simple and sublime this prayer is, how short and yet how full of whatsoever we can expect from on high.

The age at which children should make their first confession is a matter which cannot be decided here. It depends on their level of intelligence and still more on that of their conscience. We should teach them the meaning of confession as soon as they seem able to understand this. Wait therefore for the first really serious fault which a child commits. Make him feel confusion and remorse for it. As he has already been taught the meaning of confession he will naturally seek to get consolation by accusing himself to his confessor. We must try to ensure that he is stirred to a real repentance and that he may find in confession a definite easing of his trouble, so that his first confession may make a lasting impression on him and that it may become a source of grace for all his future confessions.

The first communion, on the other hand, should be made when the child, having reached the age of reason, will seem more teachable and less liable to serious faults. It is among the first-fruits of faith and the love of God that Jesus Christ makes His deepest impression through the grace of the holy communion. It should be long postponed—that is to say, we should encourage the child from his earliest years to look forward to it as the greatest blessing that one can have on earth while waiting for the joys of heaven. I believe that it should be rendered as solemn as possible, that the child should feel that on that day all eyes are fixed on him, that he is esteemed happy and that we share in his joy, and that we expect from him a conduct beyond his age in view of so great an act. But though the child should be carefully prepared for the first communion we should not anticipate too soon so precious a grace before his innocence becomes exposed to such dangerous temptations that it begins to fade.

CHAPTER IX

Remarks on some of the faults of girls

We have once more to speak of the care which must be taken to preserve girls from some of the faults which are incidental to their sex. They are brought up with a softness and diffidence which makes them incapable of a firm and well-regulated conduct. To begin with there is a good deal of affectation, and to go on with plenty of sheer habit in these ill-grounded fears and in these tears which they shed on the least provocation. Contempt for these affectations could do much to correct them, since vanity has so large a part in them.

We must also repress in them inordinate friendships, trivial jealousies, exaggerated compliments and transports. All this spoils them and accustoms them to regard as too humdrum and stiff whatever is grave and serious. We should even try to induce them to study how to speak in a short and concise manner. True intelligence is shown in cutting out any useless discourse and saying much in a few words; instead of which most women say little in many words. They take readiness of speech and vivacity of imagination for intelligence. They never make any selection among their thoughts or put them into any order with reference to what they have to explain. They are prejudiced in most of what they say and this attitude makes them talk a great deal. Meanwhile nothing good can be expected from a woman unless she can be induced to consider and examine her thoughts, to explain them in a concise manner, and to know when to be silent.

Another thing which contributes very much to the long-winded discourses of women is that they are by nature artificial and use long détours before they come to the point. They have a high opinion of craftiness—and why should they not, since they know nothing of a better kind of prudence, and this is usually the first thing that they have learnt from the example of others! They have a pliable nature which enables them to play easily all sorts of parts. Tears cost them nothing; their passions are quick and their knowledge limited. The result is that they neglect nothing in order to succeed, and methods which would not be approved by better regulated persons seem good to them. They rarely use their reason to examine whether something is desirable, yet they spare no pains in order to obtain it.

We may add that they are diffident and full of false modesty; and this again is a cause of pretence. The means to prevent so great a fault is never to give them an opportunity for being crafty, but to accustom them to say frankly what they feel about any permissible subject. They should be free to express their boredom when they feel bored. They should never be forced to appear as if they liked certain persons or books if they do not like them.

Often a mother who is biased in favour of her spiritual director[32] is displeased with her daughter if she does not submit to his direction; and the girl gives in for reasons of policy but against her own inclination. Above all never let girls suspect that you want them to aspire to become nuns;[33] for this thought destroys their confidence in their parents, suggests to them that they are not loved, agitates their minds and for years makes them feel like an un-free person. If they have been unfortunate enough to acquire the habit of concealing their feelings, the way to disabuse them is to give them sound instruction in the maxims of true prudence, just as it is obvious that the way to make them sick of the trivial stories in novels is to give them a taste for useful and interesting histories. If you do not develop in them a natural curiosity they will acquire a disordered one; and in the same way if you do not train their minds to the true prudence they will cling to the false one, which is craftiness.

Show them by examples how, without deceitfulness, one can be well-advised and diligent in the legitimate ways of being successful. Tell them that the chief part of prudence consists in speaking little and being more distrustful of oneself than of other people, but not in making false statements and being meddlesome. Uprightness of conduct and a general reputation for rectitude attract more confidence and esteem—and consequently, in the long run, more advantages, even temporal ones—than crooked methods. How clearly does this judicious rectitude mark people out and render them fit for the greatest undertakings!

But go on to say how despicable are the objects which craftiness seeks after. It is either some undesirable trifle or harmful passion. When we wish only for something lawful we desire it openly and we seek it by the right methods and with moderation. What is more pleasant or seemly than to be sincere, always calm, at peace with oneself, having nothing to fear or conceal; whereas a deceitful person is always wrought up, remorseful, in danger, and in the deplorable state of having to cover up one deception by a hundred others.

As a result of this shameful uneasiness crafty persons can never avoid the very disadvantages which they shun. Sooner or later they become known for what they really are. If they succeed in deceiving the world in some isolated instances, it is not so as regards the greater part of their life. They are always shown up in some way or other. Often they may even be the dupes of those whom they wish to deceive, for some people pretend to be dazzled by them, and they believe themselves to be esteemed even though they are really despised. But at any rate they cannot guard themselves against suspicions; and what can there be more contrary to the advantages, which a proper self-respect should aim at, than to see oneself always under suspicion? Speak of these things from time to time as occasion and need arise and in proportion to the intelligence of your hearers.

Point out again that craftiness always comes from a base heart and a mean spirit. It is clever only in trying to hide itself, doing what it ought not to do, or desiring things which are not permitted and securing them by unworthy means, not knowing how to choose the right ones. Show children the presumption of certain deceptions which they see practised and the contempt which is brought upon those who do them. In short, make them ashamed of themselves when you surprise them in any piece of deceit. From time to time deprive them of something they like because they wanted to get it by deception; and tell them that they shall have it when they ask for it openly. Do not be afraid of sympathising with their little failings, so that you may give them the courage to let these be seen. False shame is the most dangerous evil and the most urgent to cure because, if one is not careful, it renders all the others incurable.

Show them the shamefulness of that base artfulness by which one tries to make other people deceive themselves without having to reproach oneself for having deceived them. There is even more baseness and deceit in these refinements than in ordinary deception. Others may—so to speak—practise deceit honestly; but these people add a new disguise to it in order to authorise it. Tell the child that God is truth itself, and that to trifle with truth in what one says is to trifle with God. One's words should be precise and exact, and one should speak little so as to say nothing but what is right and respects the truth.

Be very careful not to imitate those people who applaud children when they have shown intelligence by some piece of deception. Far from approving of such wiles and being amused at them we should censure them severely and see that their tricks are brought to nought, so that by experience they may become disgusted with them. If you praise them for faults of this kind you will make them feel that it is clever to be deceitful.

CHAPTER X

Beauty and adornments

The chief fault to be found in girls is vanity. They are born with an eager desire to please. As the avenues which lead men to positions of authority and to glory are closed to them they try to compensate for this by graces of the mind or of the body. This explains their sweet and insinuating way of talking and why they aim so much at being beautiful, and at possessing a charming appearance, and why they are so inordinately fond of dress. A hat, a piece of ribbon, a curl of hair that is too high or too low, the choice of a colour, are for them matters of the highest importance.

This excess is more marked among our nation than in any other. The instability of disposition which is common among us causes a continual change in the fashions, so that to the love of dress is added that of novelty which has a curious attraction for the female mind. These two follies put together break down the limits set by convention and upset good manners. If there are no longer any standards for dress or house equipment there is no longer any check on anyone's social position. In the case of the domestic arrangements of any private individual the public authority has less power to intervene. Everyone chooses according to his income, or rather, if he has none, according to his ambition and vanity. This extravagance ruins families and that implies moral corruption. On the one hand it stimulates in persons of low origin the longing to become rich; and that cannot be achieved without sinning, as the Holy Spirit teaches us. On the other hand members of the higher classes, finding themselves without resources, stoop to the most despicably mean and disgraceful shifts in order to cover their expenses. In this way they gradually destroy honour, faith, honesty and good feeling, even among their nearest relations.

All these evils derive from the authority which women have of deciding about the fashions. They characterise as out-of-date those who would wish to preserve the sobriety and simplicity of old-time manners. Make an earnest endeavour therefore to help girls to understand how greatly honour depends on good conduct, and how true ability is more to be esteemed than that which is derived from one's hair or one's dress. Beauty, you will say, deceives the person who possesses it more than those who are dazzled by it. It disturbs and intoxicates the soul; one is more besotted with oneself than the most passionate lovers are with the persons whom they adore. There are only a few years of difference between one woman who is beautiful and another who is not. Beauty can only be harmful unless it can serve to marry off a daughter advantageously. But how can it do that unless it is backed up by merit and virtue? A girl can only hope to marry some young fop with whom she will be unhappy, unless her sensibleness and her modesty make her sought after by men of steady habits and solid worth. Persons who seek all their distinction from their good looks soon become ridiculous. Without noticing it they arrive at a certain age when their beauty fades and when they are still charmed with themselves, although the world, far from being so, is disgusted with them. In short, it is as unreasonable to rely solely on beauty as to place all merit in strength of body, as savage and barbarous races do.

From beauty let us pass on to the subject of clothes. True grace does not depend on vain and affected dress. It is true that one may seek elegance, shapeliness and decency in the garments which are necessary for covering our bodies; but after all these materials which cover us and can be made convenient and comfortable can never be the ornaments which confer a true beauty. I would even get girls to realise the noble simplicity that one sees in statues and other figures which remain to us of the women of Greece and Rome. They will notice in these how pleasing and majestic are full, flowing draperies and hair tied negligently behind. It would be well also if they heard mention of painters and other people[34] who have this exquisite taste for antiquity. Even if their minds were but little elevated above preoccupation with the fashions, they would soon conceive a great contempt for their artificial curls and for costumes of a too fashionable design. I am well aware that it is not desirable for them to assume an antique appearance; it would be too much to expect that; but they can, without appearing peculiar, acquire a taste for this simplicity of dress which is so dignified, gracious, and so suited to Christian manners. So, although they conform to the present custom, they will know at least that they should bear the ancient ones in mind. They will follow the fashions as a troublesome obligation and concede to them only what they cannot possibly refuse. Make them often and betimes see the vanity and frivolity which underlie the constant change of fashion. It is difficult, for example, to understand why I don't know how many head-dresses are built up to increase their stature. True grace follows nature and never spoils it.

But fashion destroys itself. It is always aiming at perfection and never attaining it; or at any rate it is never content to stop. It would be reasonable if it changed only to change no more when once it had found perfection as regards both comfort and elegance. But to go on changing for changing's sake, does not this imply seeking rather irregularity and inconstancy rather than true good manners and good taste? As a rule the fashions are a matter of caprice. Women are in a position to decide about them; it is only they who are to be believed concerning them. Thus those of them who are most shallow-minded and least educated draw the rest after them. They neither choose nor discard anything according to principle. It is enough that something has been fashionable for a long time for it to be so no longer, and for something else, however ridiculous, to take its place and be admired so long as it is considered a novelty.

After having laid this foundation show them the rules of Christian modesty. We learn, you will say, from our holy mysteries that man is born in the corruption of sin. His body being infected with a contagious disease is an inexhaustible source of temptations for the soul. Jesus

Christ teaches us to place all our virtue in the fear and distrust of self. Would you wish, you could say to a girl, to endanger your own soul and that of your neighbour for the sake of a foolish vanity? Be horrified therefore at these bare necks and other immodesties. Even if these faults are committed without any evil passion they are at any rate due to vanity and an immoderate desire to please. Does this vanity justify in the sight of God and man a conduct so reckless, so scandalous and so dangerous to others? Is this blind desire to please becoming to a Christian soul which ought to regard as idolatry whatever diverts it from the love of the Creator and the contempt of creatures? But when you seek to please what is it that you are meaning to do? Is it not to excite the passions of men? You have the power of controlling them, but if they go too far can one not expect all the consequences? And do they not in fact always go too far once they have been kindled? You are preparing a subtle and deadly poison. You pour this on all who see you, and yet you think yourself innocent. Go on to quote examples of women whose modesty has made them worthy of commendation and of those whose lack of it has damaged their reputation. But above all never allow girls to dress above their rank. Censure severely all their fancies and show them the danger to which they are exposing themselves and how they make themselves despised by sensible people if they forget their position.

What remains to do is to guard girls against trying to appear clever. If they are not careful when they are to any extent vivacious they will always be meddling and ready to talk about everything. They lay down the law on matters quite beyond their capacity and affect to be bored by exactness. A girl ought not to speak unless it is really necessary, and even then with an air of hesitance and diffidence. She ought not to speak about matters which are above the ordinary reach of girls, even though she has had some instruction in them. Although she may have as much as she wants of memory, vivaciousness, tricks of speech and the ability to talk pleasantly, all these qualities she shares with a large number of other women who have little sense and are very contemptible. But her behaviour should be well-regulated; she should have a well-balanced and steadfast disposition; she should know when to keep silent and how to manage things—a quality so rare that it will mark her out among the members of her sex. But as for fastidiousness and affectation they must be repressed, by showing that good taste consists in accommodating oneself to affairs according as they are more or less useful.

Nothing is really estimable except good sense and virtue. Together they make one realise that distaste and boredom are not to be regarded as a praiseworthy refinement, but as the weakness of a disordered mind. Since we have to live among unrefined persons and to take part in occupations which are not very attractive, reason which alone secures refinement helps us to be unrefined with those who are so. A mind which can appreciate good manners, but can raise itself at need above them so as to attain more worthy aims, is infinitely superior to that fussy kind of disposition which is the slave of its own dislikes.

CHAPTER XI

The duties of women

We come now to the details of those matters in which a woman should be instructed. What are her occupations? She has the duty of educating her children—the boys up to a certain age and girls until they get married or take the veil. She has the supervision of the servants, with their manners and duties. She must see to the details of household expenditure and to the means of doing everything economically and honourably; and usually she must also look after leases and the receiving of rents.[35] The limits of a woman's learning—like that of a man—should be determined by her duties. The difference in their studies should be conditioned by the difference in their occupations. A woman's instruction therefore should be restricted to the matters which we have mentioned. But a curious woman may find that this sets too narrow limits to her curiosity. She is wrong. The fact is that she does not recognise the importance and extent of the matters in which I propose that she should be instructed.

What a discerning judgment she will need in order to understand the nature and aptitudes of each of her children, to find out the right way of treating them and to discover their dispositions, their propensities, their talents; to check their rising passions, to instil into them good principles, to amend their errors! What prudence she will need to gain and maintain authority over them without losing their friendship and confidence! But does she not also need to watch and know thoroughly the persons with whom she puts them in contact? Doubtless a mother of a family ought to be fully instructed in religion and have an understanding which is mature, steadfast, diligent and experienced in government.

Can it be doubted that women are charged with all these duties, since they naturally devolve on them even during the lifetime of their husbands if they are occupied away from home? They concern them still more closely if they become widows. St Paul associates their salvation so much with the education of their children that he asserts that through this they will be saved.

I do not explain here everything which women ought to do in connection with the education of their children, because this reminder will be sufficient to make them realise the extent of the knowledge which they should have.

To the control of children estate-management should be added. Most women neglect it as being a mean employment suited only to peasants or farmers, or at best to a steward or housekeeper. In particular women who have been bred up to a life of ease, luxury and indolence are careless and disdainful of any details of this kind. They make no great difference between life in the country and that of the savages in Canada. If you speak to them of the price of corn, of the cultivation of the land, of different kinds of estates, of the collecting of rents and other dues of a landowner, of the best way of managing a lease or of appointing collectors, they think that you want to reduce them to employments quite unworthy of them. Yet it is only through ignorance that one despises this art of estate-management. The ancient Greeks and Romans, who were so skilful and so refined, instructed themselves in it with the greatest care. The chief men among them, out of their own experience, composed books which we still possess in which they dealt with agriculture[36] in a most detailed fashion. We know too that their conquerors did not disdain to till the ground and to return to the plough[37] after celebrating a triumph. This is so far removed from our present-day customs that we should not believe it were there not in history no reason to doubt it. But is it not as natural to cultivate one's land peaceably as to think of defending it or extending it by force? What is the good of victory except to gather the fruits of peace? After all, soundness of understanding consists in endeavouring to be exactly instructed as to the way in which those things are done which are fundamental to human existence. All the most important issues depend on this. The power and honour of a state consist not in possessing many ill-cultivated provinces, but in deriving from the lands which it does possess whatever is needful for easily supporting a numerous population.

It is doubtless necessary to have a much higher and more developed intelligence in order to be instructed in all the arts related to estate-management, and to be in a position to organise a whole household, which is like a little republic, than to play at cards or gossip about the fashions or be concerned with making pretty little speeches. It is a very contemptible sort of disposition which aims at nothing beyond speaking acceptably. One is always meeting women whose conversation is full of sensible remarks, but whose conduct, through lack of having applied themselves betimes, is simply frivolous.

But guard against the opposite fault. Women run the risk of going to extremes in everything. It is good to accustom them from childhood to carry some responsibility, to keep their accounts, to note the details of whatever is bought and to know the proper use of everything. Be careful too that estate-management with them does not degenerate into avarice. Show them the absurdity of this failing. Bid them beware lest avarice grows a little but brings great dishonour. A reasonable person by means of a simple and industrious life should try to avoid the disgrace and injustice inherent in an extravagant and ruinous one. The only reason for economising on unnecessary expenses is to be able more liberally to incur those which are prompted by friendship or charity. It is often a great gain to know when it is proper to lose. It is good management and not sordid economics that brings in the best profits. Do not fail to point out the arrant folly of those women who are intent on saving a candle-end while allowing themselves to be cheated by a steward in the management of their estates.

Treat the subject of neatness in the same way as that of house-management. Never allow girls to have anything soiled or untidy. Get them to notice the least disorder in the house, and to realise that nothing contributes more to good housekeeping and neatness than to have everything in its proper place. This rule may seem very trivial, but it will have important consequences if it is strictly kept. If you have need of anything you will not lose a minute in finding it. There will not be any trouble or dispute or confusion; you can put your hand on it immediately and when you have finished with it you can put it straight back in the place from which you have taken it. Good order is one of the chief elements in neatness. Seeing everything so exactly arranged is what most attracts attention. Besides, putting everything in its most suitable place, not only for seemliness and attractiveness but also for keeping it safe, means that it is less soon worn out. It is not so liable to be spoiled by some accident and it is more neatly kept. For example, a piece of crockery will not get so dusty or in danger of being broken if one puts it back in its place immediately after using it. The habit of precision which leads us to keep things tidy also helps us to keep them clean. This habit has also the advantage of keeping servants from being idle and untidy. Again, it helps to make them render their service promptly and readily, and to take away from oneself the temptation of being impatient at delays which arise from things being out of place so that they cannot be found. At the same time do not overdo fastidiousness and neatness. Neatness in moderation is a virtue, but when one exaggerates it, it degenerates into pettiness. Good taste rejects excessive fussiness. It treats trivial matters as such and is not worried about them. Therefore in the presence of children laugh at the baubles which some women find so attractive and which lead them into such foolish expenditure. Accustom them to a kind of neatness which is simple and easy to practise. Show them the best way of doing things, but at the same time the advantage of not being dependent on them. Tell them how petty and mean it is to complain about a soup not properly seasoned or a badly folded curtain or a chair which is too high or too low.

It is doubtless the mark of a better disposition to be purposely unrefined, rather than to be over-fastidious about matters of little importance. This blameworthy fastidiousness, if it is not corrected in women of intelligence, is particularly dangerous in conversations with other persons. Most of these appear dull and uninteresting to them. The least lack of politeness seems monstrous to them and they are always scornful and disgusted. They must be made to understand betimes that there is nothing so injudicious as to judge anyone superficially by his manners, instead of thoroughly examining his character, his views and his useful qualities. Make them see, by various examples, how that a countryman with an unrefined, or (if you like) a ridiculous, manner, with his inept compliments, if he has an honest heart and a well-regulated mind, is more to be esteemed than a courtier who under cover of the most accomplished politeness hides an ungrateful and unjust heart and is capable of any sort of treachery and baseness.[38] Add that there is always weakness in those characters which are much inclined to boredom and fastidiousness. There are hardly any people whose conversation is so bad but that something good can be extracted from it, though one should choose the best when one is free to do so. We can console ourselves, if we are reduced to it, by talking to them about the things they know, and persons of intelligence can always derive some kind of instruction from those who are less educated. But let us return to the matters in which a girl should be instructed.

CHAPTER XII

The duties of women (*continued*)

There is an art in being served and it is not unimportant. One should select servants who are honest and religious. The duties which are assigned to them, the time and care to be devoted to each of these, and the expense thereby incurred, must all be made clear. For example, it would be absurd to scold a servant if you wanted him to have prepared some dish sooner than it was possible to do this, or if you do not know roughly the price and quantity of the sugar and other ingredients which are to be used in what you want made. In that way you would risk becoming either the dupe or the bane of your domestics if you have not some knowledge of their duties. One should also understand their dispositions and know how to deal with them tactfully, and order your little republic which is only too often unruly. Authority is certainly needed, for the less reasonable people are, the more necessary it is to hold them in check by fear; but since your servants are Christians and your brethren in Jesus Christ and you should respect them as His members, you must make use of authority only when persuasion fails.

Try then to make yourself beloved of your servants without any undue familiarity. Do not enter into conversation with them, but at the same time do not hesitate to speak to them fairly often concerning their needs in a friendly way and without haughtiness. Let them feel sure that they can come to you for advice and compassion. Do not reprehend them sharply for their faults, and do not appear either surprised or put out by these, so long as you can hope that they are not incurable. Help them to understand reason calmly, and often put up with the faults in their service so that they may realise that you are speaking to them dispassionately, without annoyance or impatience, and much less for your own service than for their interest. It will not be easy to accustom young persons of high birth to behave in this gentle and charitable way, for the impatience and impetuosity of youth, joined to the false ideas which their birth gives them, makes them regard servants almost like horses. They think themselves of a different nature from that of footmen, and regard them as having been made for the convenience of their masters. Show how contrary these ideas are to modesty and respect for one's neighbour. Make it clear that men are not made to be waited on and that it is a shocking error to believe that some men are born to pander to the idleness and pride of others. As service has been established contrary to natural equality among men it should be alleviated as much as possible. Since masters, who are better educated than their servants, are themselves full of faults they must not expect the latter to have none, since they have not had the benefit of instruction and good examples. In short if domestics injure themselves by doing their service badly, what is usually called being well served injures their masters still more, because this easiness of having all one's whims humoured and all one's wishes fulfilled only weakens the soul and makes it eager and greedy for the slightest opportunities to indulge its desires.

As to this household management nothing is better than to accustom girls to it betimes. Give them something to be responsible for on condition that they must render account of it to you. This trust will delight them, for young people feel an inexpressible pleasure if you begin to put confidence in them and introduce them to some serious undertaking. There is a remarkable example of this in the case of Queen Marguerite.[39] This princess relates in her *Mémoires* how the keenest pleasure of her life was to feel that the Queen, her mother, was beginning to talk to her, though she was still quite young, as if she were a mature person. She was delighted to be admitted to the confidence of the Queen and her brother, the Duke of Anjou, in the matter of state secrets—she who had hitherto known nothing more than children's play. Even suffer a girl to commit a few faults in these first attempts, and put up with something in instructing her. Get her to realise calmly what she ought to have done or said in order to avoid the difficulties in which she has landed herself. Relate to her your own past experiences and do not hesitate to tell her of the faults, similar to her own, which you committed in your youth. In this way you will gain her confidence without which education becomes a mere succession of disagreeable formalities.

Teach a girl to read and write correctly. It is shameful—but quite usual—to find women who have intelligence and good manners, but who cannot pronounce correctly what they read. They either hesitate or else read in a sing-song manner; whereas one should pronounce in a simple and natural, though steady and controlled, tone of voice. They are still more deficient as regards spelling[40] or in the manner of forming and connecting their letters when they are writing. At least accustom girls to keep their lines straight and to make their letters clear and legible. A girl should also know the grammar of her native language. It is not a question of teaching it to her by rule, as schoolboys learn Latin. Simply accustom her without any affectation not to take one tense for another, to make use of the proper grammatical terms, to set forth her thoughts in an orderly, concise and definite manner. You will set her in the way of being able one day to teach her own children to speak well without any formal study. We know that in ancient Rome the mother of the Gracchi contributed, by the education which she gave her sons, to forming their powers of eloquence when they became men.

Girls ought also to know the four rules of arithmetic. You will make good use of these when teaching them to keep accounts. Many people find this a troublesome business; but if the habit is acquired in childhood and plenty of practice is given in dealing with complicated accounts by the help of rules, this dislike will be largely overcome. It is well known that being able to keep exact accounts often conduces to the effective running of a household.

It would be advisable also that they should know something of the chief principles of law, as for example the difference between a will and a donation, what is meant by contract, entail and partition among co-heirs, the chief rules of the law and customs of the region in which one lives and which render these acts valid, the nature of property, the meaning of joint estate, the difference between moveable and fixed chattels. If they get married all their chief concerns will turn upon matters of this kind. But at the same time show them how incapable they are of plunging into legal difficulties, and how the law itself, owing to the weakness of human capacity, is full of obscurities and pitfalls; how the law varies and becomes uncertain and how much it depends upon judicial interpretation even if it may seem clear; how often the dragging out of even the most favourable cases[41] may lead to annoyance and ruin. Show them the bustle and sharp practice of the law-court, the subtleties of legal procedure, the immense expense involved, the unhappiness of those who plead, the keenness of solicitors, attorneys and clerks to get rich by impoverishing their clients. Refer also to the ways by which a cause which in itself is good is rendered bad by the way in which it is presented, and the opposition between the rules of one court and another. If you go to the *Grand' Chambre*[42] your action is gained; if you go to the *Chambre des Enquêtes* it is lost. Remember the conflicts of jurisdiction and the risk of pleading for several years before the *Conseil d'État* merely to find out where one ought to plead. Finally mark the difference that is frequently found between one counsel or judge and another in the same case. In the consultation you may gain your cause, but the verdict may condemn you to pay damages.

All this makes me feel that it is important to prevent women, who are widows or mistresses of their own estates, from getting too much concerned about going to law or surrendering too blindly to advisers who are against coming to terms. They should listen to their men of business but not put themselves in their power. They should be on their guard when entering upon a lawsuit and should consult experienced men who are inclined towards the advantages of arranging a compromise; and finally they should be persuaded that the wisest course in these affairs is to foresee the inconveniences and know how to avoid them.

Girls of high birth and considerable fortune should be instructed in the duties of a lord of the manor. Tell them therefore what steps it is necessary to take to prevent the abuse, violence, trickery and duplicity which are common in country districts. Describe the ways of setting up elementary schools[43] and charitable organisations for the relief of the sick and poor. Show also the industries which can sometimes be established in certain areas for the diminution of poverty, and above all the means by which one can secure for the peasantry a sound instruction and a truly christian régime. To describe all this would involve greater detail than can be dealt with here. But in explaining the duties of the landed gentry one should not forget their rights. Tell them what is meant by *fiefs*,[44] *seigneur dominant*, *vassal*, *hommage*, *rentes*, *dîmes inféodées*, *droit de champart*, *lods et ventes*, *indemnités*, *amortissement et reconnoissances*, *papiers terriers*, and other similar terms. A knowledge of them is necessary because the management of one's estates is entirely concerned with them.

After these instructions, which should come first, I think it is useful to allow girls, according to their leisure and their intellectual aptitude, to read such secular works as are not dangerous as regards the passions. This is a way of giving them a distaste for comedies and novels. Give them therefore the histories of Greece and Rome. In them they will see examples of outstanding courage and self-denial. Do not leave them ignorant of the history of France which has also its attractions; add that of other neighbouring countries, with descriptions of distant lands judiciously treated. All this will serve to elevate their minds and stimulate them to noble thoughts, provided that vanity and affectation be avoided.

It is commonly thought that a high-born girl should learn Italian and Spanish, but I can see no value in this study unless a girl is going to be attached to the household of some Spanish or Italian princess, such as our queens Anne of Austria and Catherine de' Medici.[45] Otherwise these two languages are useful for little else than reading dangerous books which will be likely to increase a woman's faults. There is much more to be lost than gained in this study. The learning of Latin is much more reasonable. It is the language of the Church and there is an immense advantage and satisfaction in being able to understand the words of the Divine Office, at which one assists so often. Even those who are looking for beauty of language will find it far more perfectly and soundly expressed in Latin than in Italian or Spanish where wit and liveliness of imagination run riot. But I would teach Latin only to such girls as have a sound judgment and are well-conducted, who know how to undertake this study for its own value and not through vain curiosity, who will not display what they have learnt and seek in it only their own edification.

I would also allow them, though with careful selection, the reading of rhetorical and poetical works if I saw that they had a taste for them and if their judgment was sufficiently sound to restrict them to the proper use of such material. But I would beware of over-exciting their imagination and in all this I should like a true restraint. Anything which has a love interest, the more it is glozed over and wrapped up the more dangerous I think it is.

With music and painting the same precautions are necessary. All the arts imply the same spirit and the same taste. As for music we know that the ancients thought that there was nothing more dangerous to a well-governed state than the introduction of an effeminate type of music.[46] It enervates men and renders them soft and given to pleasure. Languishing and passionate airs are so alluring only because the soul surrenders itself to the charm of the senses and becomes intoxicated with it. For this reason the magistrates at Sparta used to break all instruments whose music was too attractive, and this was one of their most important duties. For this reason Plato also severely rejected all those enervating modes which came from Asia. For an even stronger reason Christians, who ought never to seek pleasure merely for pleasure's sake, should abominate these poisonous amusements.

Poetry and music, if we exclude whatever does not conduce to their true aim, can be very usefully employed to excite in the mind lively and lofty sentiments leading to virtue. How many poetical works there are in Scripture, which apparently used to be sung by the Hebrews! Songs were the first repository, earlier than writing itself, which preserved even more definitely the tradition of things divine among men. We have seen how among heathen people music had power to raise the soul above base thoughts. The Church has thought that the best way to comfort her children is by singing the praises of God. We cannot therefore reject these arts which the Spirit of God Himself has consecrated. Music and poetry, if they be Christian, would be the greatest of all aids to induce disgust with profane pleasures; but owing to the wrong attitude[47] towards these arts which is fashionable in our present society, a taste for them is not without danger. So we should lose no time in showing a young lady, who is susceptible to the influence of music, how much charm there can be in it even if one confines oneself to sacred compositions. If she can sing and appreciate the beauties of music do not hope to keep her for ever ignorant of them. Prohibition will only increase her enthusiasm for them. It is much better to give an orderly course to this torrent than to try to stop it.

Design can easily be made a beneficial art, and besides it is particularly suited to women, for without it their needlework cannot be satisfactorily carried out. I know that they could confine themselves to plain pieces of work which do not call for a knowledge of art; but it seems to me if design is needed it exercises both the mind and the hands of a lady of quality; and I hope that she would produce work in which art and industry alike would season her occupation with a certain pleasure. Such work cannot have any true beauty if the rules of design are neglected; and so it is that practically every piece of material or lace or embroidery that one sees nowadays is in bad taste. Everything is confused, badly designed, out of proportion. These things are considered fine because they cost a good deal of labour to those who make them and of money to those who buy them. Their brilliance dazzles those who see them from a distance or who cannot judge them properly. Women have made their rules governing these fashions, and if anyone disputes them he is thought not to know what he is talking about. Yet they could disabuse themselves if they considered the principles of design and thereby fit themselves to produce, at small expense and yet with great pleasure, pieces of work in noble variety and of a beauty far above that of the arbitrary fashions.

Girls should shun and despise idleness. Let them remember that the early Christians, of whatever class they were, worked not just to amuse themselves but to make of their work a serious, steady and useful occupation. The natural order of things, the punishment visited on Adam and through him on all his descendants, the example set by the second Adam which is Jesus Christ—all this obliges us to a laborious life, each in his own sphere.

In considering the education of a girl one should take into account her position in society, the places where she is destined to spend her life and the occupation which she is likely to take up. Be careful that she does not cherish hopes which are above her fortune and condition. There is hardly anyone who has not had to suffer for setting his hopes too high; what might have rendered him happy only makes him discontented. If a girl has to live in the country let her be brought up early to those occupations which she will have there, and do not let her sample the amusements of the town. Show her the advantages of a plain and active life, and keep her away from people who are attached to the Court. Contact with them will only tempt her to put on silly and unbecoming airs. Keep her within the bounds of her own position in society and set her as models the persons who succeed best there. Adapt her mind to those duties which she will have to perform all her life long. Teach her how to manage a bourgeois household, and the care which she must have for the revenues of a country estate or the rents from houses in town, as well as all that pertains to the education of children; and in short all the details of the other duties which she is bound to undertake if she gets married. If on the contrary she makes up her mind to become a nun, without being persuaded into it by her parents, direct all her education thenceforward towards the state to which she is aspiring. Get her to try out seriously the powers of her mind and her body, without waiting for the noviciate, which is a kind of engagement like giving one's word of honour in worldly affairs. Accustom her to silence, inure her to obedience in matters contrary to her desires or what she is used to. Try to find out by degrees how far she is adapted to the rule of the Order which she wishes to enter. Endeavour to accustom her to a hard, stern and laborious life. Show her in detail how free and happy one is to feel able to do without the things which vanity and idleness, or even the usages of polite society, render necessary outside the cloister. In a word, by getting her to practise poverty make her realise the happiness which Jesus Christ has revealed to us. Finally, neglect nothing which will remove from her heart any vanity of the world when once she will leave it. Without making her undergo any experience which might prove too dangerous, show her the thorns hidden beneath the pleasures which the world gives, and how people can be wretched there in the midst of pleasures.

CHAPTER XIII

Governesses

I foresee that my plan of education may be regarded by many people as a chimerical project. It will be said that, in order to achieve it, a judgment, a patience and an aptitude far beyond the ordinary will be necessary. Where are the governesses capable of understanding it? Even more, where are those who can carry it out? But please consider that when one undertakes a work dealing with the best kind of education which can be given to children it is no good recommending half measures. So it should not be taken amiss if in one's investigation one aims at what is most perfect. It is true that everyone may not be able to reach as far as my suggestions go, but there is nothing to stop my putting them down on paper. Even if one cannot attain perfection in the work, it will not be useless to know what it is and to be forced to aim at it. This is the best way of approaching it. Again, this task does not imply a complete knowledge of childhood, and a combination of all the most favourable circumstances for achieving a perfect education. On the contrary I am trying to prescribe remedies for natures which are depraved or spoilt. I envisage the ordinary setbacks and I have recourse to the simplest methods of putting right, either wholly or in part, whatever needs this. It is true that in this little treatise you will not find how to make a neglected or badly conducted education turn out well. But need you be astonished at that? Is not the discovery of simple rules, the carrying out of which will ensure a sound education, the best that one can hope for? I confess that one can do—every day one does—much less for children than I have proposed; but on the other hand it is only too obvious how much young people suffer through negligence. The way which I have described, however long it seems, is really the shortest and leads straight to the goal. The other way, which is that of fear and superficial culture of the mind, however short it seems, is too long, because by it one hardly ever arrives at the true end of education which is to influence children's minds and inspire them with the true love of virtue. Most children who have been led by this way will have to begin all over again when their education is finished; and after they have spent the first years after their entry into society in committing faults which are often irreparable, they must, by experience and reflection, realise the truth of those rules which a faulty and superficial education would never have instilled into them. It should be noted that this initial trouble which we should take with regard to children, and which inexperienced people regard as burdensome and impracticable, will obviate much worse annoyances and will straighten out difficulties which, in the course of an education less exact and more severe, would ultimately prove insurmountable. Lastly, consider that in order to carry out this educational project the concern is not so much for doing things which require a great talent, but for avoiding the glaring faults which I have dealt with here in detail. Often it is only a question of not pressing children too much, of taking great care of them, of observing them and winning their confidence, of replying clearly and sensibly to their little questions, of letting them act according to their nature so that one can the better understand it, and of putting them right with patience when they are misled or at fault.

It is not to be expected that a good education can be

imparted by a bad governess. Doubtless it is sufficient to lay down rules which will make it successful in the hands of an ordinary person. It is not asking too much to expect of her some measure of good sense, a teachable disposition and a true fear of God. Such a governess will find in this treatise nothing too profound or too abstract. Even if she does not understand everything she will perceive the main points and that will suffice. Get her to read it several times and take the trouble to read it over with her. Allow her to stop you whenever there is anything which she does not understand or of which she does not feel fully convinced. Then set her to work, and if you find that when speaking to the child she loses sight of the rules laid down in this treatise and which she ought to follow, talk to her gently about this in private. Taking all this trouble may at first be wearisome, but if you are the child's father or mother it is your fundamental duty. Moreover you will not for long have serious difficulties in this respect, because if your governess is sensible and willing she will learn more in a month by practice and your advice than by long arguments. She will soon be able to go in the right way of her own initiative. You will also have a chance of being relieved, because she will find in this little work the chief explanations which one should give children on the most important points, fully dealt with and which she has only to follow. She will thus have before her eyes a collection of conversations which she should have with children concerning those matters which are most difficult for them to understand. This is a kind of practical education which will, as it were, lead her by the hand. You can also very advantageously make use of the *Historical Catechism*[48] of which I have already spoken. Get the governess, whom you are training, to read it several times, and in particular to understand the preface properly so that she may have full knowledge of this method of teaching. It must however be confessed that persons even of ordinary ability, to whom I confine my remarks, are not easy to find, and that it is necessary therefore to have some specific method of education, seeing that the simplest things do not just happen of themselves and that they are always done badly by the wrong kind of person. Choose therefore either from your own household or from your estates or among your friends or in some well-conducted convent a girl who seems capable of being trained. Endeavour to fit her betimes for this occupation and keep her under your own observation for a time in order to test her before you entrust to her something so precious. Five or six governesses trained in this way would soon be capable of training a large number of others. Perhaps some of them would be disappointing, but in the long run there would always be enough to compensate and one would not be in the present state of difficulty. Regular and secular communities also which are dedicated to the education of girls will also be able to adopt my recommendations in training their *maîtresses de pensionnaires* and *maîtresses d'école*.[49]

But though the difficulty of finding governesses is great it must be confessed that there is another still greater—and that is the irregular conduct of parents. Everything else is useless if they do not also co-operate in this task. The principal thing is that they should set their children high standards and good examples. This can be hoped for in only a very few families. As a rule in great households one sees nothing but confusion, change, and a crowd of servants all at loggerheads among themselves and with their masters. What an appalling school for children! Often a mother, who spends her time gaming[50] or at the theatre or in indecorous conversation, will complain in serious tones that she cannot find a governess fit to bring up her daughters. But what could the best education do for a girl with the example of such a mother? Often one sees parents who (as St Augustine says) take their children to public shows and other entertainments which cannot fail to make them discontented with a serious and active life, and in which the parents themselves may wish them to take part. Thus they mingle poison with wholesome fare. They talk about wisdom, but they accustom the volatile imagination of children to the violent agitations produced by emotional plays or music; and after that they cannot settle down to study. They give them the taste for unbridled emotions and make them consider innocent pleasures as insipid. After this they still expect education to succeed, and they regard it as dull and harsh if it does not admit of this mixture of good and evil. Does not this imply that one is trying to get the honour of seeking a good education for one's children, but is not willing to take pains about it or submit to the most necessary rules for securing it?

Let us conclude with the portrait which the Wise Man makes of the Virtuous Woman.[51] Her price, he says, is like that which cometh from afar, from the ends of the earth. The heart of her husband doth safely trust in her, so that he shall have no need of spoil. She will do him good and not evil all the days of her life. She seeketh wool and flax and worketh willingly with her hands. She is like the merchants' ships; she bringeth her food from afar. She riseth while it is yet night and giveth meat to her household and a portion to her maidens. She considereth a field and buyeth it; with the fruit of her hands she planteth a vineyard. She girdeth her loins with strength and strengtheneth her arms. She perceiveth that her merchandise is good; her candle goeth not out by night. She layeth her hands to the spindle and her hands hold the distaff. She stretcheth out her hand to the poor; yea, she reacheth forth her hands to the needy. She is not afraid of the snow for her household, for all her household are clothed with scarlet. She maketh herself coverings of tapestry; her clothing is silk and purple. Her husband is known in the gates when he sitteth among the elders of the land. She maketh fine linen and selleth it, and delivereth girdles unto the merchant. Strength and honour are her clothing and she shall rejoice in time to come. She openeth her mouth with wisdom, and in her tongue is the law of kindness. She looketh well to the ways of her household and eateth not the bread of idleness. Her children arise up and call her blessed, her husband also, and he praiseth her. Many daughters have done virtuously, but thou excellest them all. Favour is deceitful and beauty is vain; but a woman that feareth the Lord, she shall be praised. Give her of the fruit of her hands, and let her own works praise her in the gate.

Although the extreme differences of customs and the conciseness and boldness of the expressions tend to make this kind of language at first obscure, yet there can be found in it a style so vivid and pregnant that one is soon charmed with it if one examines it closely. But what I would emphasise here is the authority of Solomon, the wisest of men—nay, it is that of the Holy Spirit Himself whose words are so splendidly adapted to make us admire, even in a rich and high-born woman, simplicity of manners, good house-management and hard work.

ADVICE from M. DE FÉNELON, Archbishop of Cambrai, to a LADY OF QUALITY, concerning the EDUCATION OF HER DAUGHTER

In accordance with your wish, Madame, I will lay before you my ideas with regard to the education of your daughter.

If you had several daughters you might perhaps be excused this trouble in view of your many outside duties which are greater than you might desire. In that case you could choose a good convent where the boarders are carefully educated. But since you have only one girl[52] to bring up and God has given you the opportunity of taking charge of her I think that you can give her a better education than any convent can. The eyes of a wise, loving and Christian mother can, no doubt, discern what other people cannot see. Because this gift is very rare the best course for mothers is to entrust convents with the task of educating their daughters, because they themselves often lack the knowledge necessary for this task. Or even if they do possess it they do not back it up by a serious, Christian way of life, without which the soundest instruction makes no impression; for everything which such a mother tells her daughter is counteracted by what the girl sees her do. That is not the case with you, Madame. Your only aim is to serve God. Religion is the first of your concerns, and you will inspire in your daughter that which she sees you practise. For this reason I exempt you from the general rule, and I prefer you to educate her rather than any convent. It is also a great advantage in the education which you give her to have her near you. If a convent is not well ordered she will see there vanity held in honour, and this is the subtlest of all poisons for a young person. There she will hear the world spoken of as a kind of enchanted place, and nothing makes a more pernicious impression than this false idea of the world which is regarded from afar with admiration, and the pleasures of which are exaggerated without showing its disappointments and sorrows. The world never dazzles so much as when one sees it from a distance and never close up, and without any warning against its deceits. For this reason I distrust a worldly convent even more than the world itself. If on the other hand a convent is full of religious zeal and keeps the rules of its Order faithfully, a girl of high birth grows up there in complete ignorance of the world outside. This is doubtless a happy ignorance if it is to go on for ever. But if this girl leaves the convent and at a certain age goes back to her father's house where the world confronts her, nothing is more to be feared than the resulting surprise and shock to a vivid imagination. A girl who has been shut off from the world simply by letting her know nothing about it, and in whom virtue is not as yet strongly rooted, is soon tempted to believe that whatever is most wonderful has hitherto been hidden from her. She leaves the convent like a person brought up in the darkness of a deep cavern who is suddenly taken out into the light of day. Nothing gives a greater shock than this unexpected transition and this glare to which one has not been accustomed. It would be much better to accustom a girl gradually to the world under the guidance of a wise and religious mother who will show her only so much of it as is fitting for her to see, who will point out its faults when they occur, and who will set her the example of making use of it only in moderation and so far as is necessary. I have a high opinion of the education given in good convents; but I count still more on that given by a good mother if she is free to take on this work. I conclude therefore, Madame, that your daughter is better with you than in the best convent that you could choose. But there are few mothers to whom one should give a piece of advice like this.

It is true that there are great risks in this kind of education if you are not careful to choose suitable women to be in your daughter's company. Your duties at home and your charitable works abroad do not allow you to have your child always under your eyes. It is desirable that she should leave you as little as possible, but you will not be able to take her with you everywhere. If you leave her to women of a frivolous, ill-regulated and indiscreet character[53] they will do her more harm in a week than the good which you could do her in several years. These persons who themselves have as a rule received a bad education will gradually give her a similar one. They will talk too freely among themselves in the presence of the child who notices everything and wants to imitate it. They will express views which are false and dangerous. The child will hear them talk scandal, lie, suspect on inadequate grounds, criticise without justification. She will see jealousy and unfriendliness, whimsical and inconsistent behaviour, sometimes devotions which are insincere or superstitious or irregular, and her most serious faults will go uncorrected. Moreover, people of a servile disposition will not fail to try to please the child by humouring or flattering her in a most dangerous way. I admit that education in the most mediocre convent is better than this kind of home education. But I take it that you will never lose sight of your daughter except in case of absolute necessity, and that you will at least have a reliable person who will be responsible for her on the occasions when you are forced to leave her. It is essential that this person should have enough good sense and virtue to be able to exercise a kindly authority, which will keep the other women up to their duties, to call the child to order if need be without incurring her dislike, and to report to you whatever needs looking into. I confess that such a woman is not easy to find; but it is of the first importance to try to discover her and to spare no expense in making her position with you comfortable. I know that one may encounter many disappointments; but one has to be contented with the essential qualifications and put up with the faults which are mingled with them. Unless you have such a person ready to help you, you cannot hope to succeed.

Since your daughter shows considerable intelligence and has a quick, ready and acute mind I fear she may become affected and develop a vain and dangerous excess of curiosity. You will allow me, Madame, if you please, to add that this should not offend you because you are not in any way responsible. Women are usually even more keen on the adornments of the mind than on those of the body. Those who are capable of study and hope to distinguish themselves thereby, have even more enthusiasm for their books than for their clothes. They conceal their knowledge a little—but they only half conceal it so as to gain credit for modesty as well as ability. Other more crude forms of vanity are more easily corrected because they are noticed and censured and they are the mark of a frivolous character. But a woman of an inquiring mind, who sets up for knowing a great deal, prides herself on being an outstanding genius among her sex. She thinks it fine to despise the vain amusements of other women. She thinks she is always right and nothing will cure her of this obstinacy. As a rule she can never but half know anything. She is more dazzled than enlightened by what she knows. She flatters herself that she knows everything and can make the decisions. She becomes a passionate partisan of one party against another in all the disputes which take place, even in matters of religion. This is the reason why all these new-fangled sects[54] have made so much headway owing to the women who have introduced and supported them. Women are eloquent in conversation and active in carrying on an intrigue. The gross vanity of women who are recognised as vain is less to be feared than the serious and refined vanity of those who aim at being highly intelligent in order to shine with a mere show of true merit. It is therefore of the first importance always to recall your daughter to a reasonable simplicity. It suffices if she knows enough about religion to believe it and to carry it out properly in practice, without ever arguing about it. She must listen only to the Church and not become a follower of some proscribed preacher or someone suspected of innovations. Her spiritual director must be a man who is openly opposed to anything which is called a sect. She must avoid conversing with women who meddle with rash arguments concerning doctrine, and she must realise how unbecoming and dangerous this freedom is. She should have a horror of pernicious books, without wanting to find out what it is in them that makes them forbidden. She must learn to distrust herself and to beware of the snares of curiosity and presumption. She must learn to pray to God in all humility, to become poor in spirit, to meditate often, to obey without respite, to allow herself to be corrected even in her most fixed ideas by experienced persons who are fond of her, and to hold her peace and allow others to do the talking. I would rather she should know all about your major-domo's accounts than about the theologian's discussions on Grace.[55] Keep her busy with a piece of needlework that will be useful in your house and which will accustom her to avoid dangerous relations with the outside world. But never let her argue about theology to the great danger of her faith. Everything is lost if she obstinately tries to be clever and gets a distaste for domestic duties. The virtuous woman spins, confines herself to her home, keeps quiet, believes and obeys; she does not argue against the Church.

I am quite sure, Madame, that you will know how to introduce, when occasion offers, some reflections on the immodesty and lack of principle which are found in some women of high intelligence, so that you may help your daughter to avoid this danger. But as the authority of a mother runs the risk of wearing out and as the wisest of lessons do not always convince a girl against her will, I hope that women of high reputation in society, who are among your friends, will talk with you in the presence of this young lady and without appearing to be concerned with her, in order to censure the vain and foolish behaviour of women who affect to be highly educated and who hanker after innovations in religion. These indirect lessons, it appears, make more impression than all that you can say to her directly when you are alone together.

As regards dress I hope that you will be able to give your daughter a taste for true moderation. There is a type of woman who goes to extremes and who cannot endure the happy mean. They would prefer to have a plain austerity if this were the mark of some striking change of fashion, rather than to keep to the middle way which they despise as being characteristic of lack of taste and a dull disposition. It remains true that it is most praiseworthy, though very rare, to find a wise and moderate character which avoids these two extremes and which, while conceding to the proprieties that which one cannot refuse them, never oversteps the limit. True wisdom in the matter of furniture, household gear and clothes, is to have nothing that calls for comment, either good or bad. Let it be enough, you will say to your daughter, to avoid being criticised as a person lacking in taste or untidy or slovenly; but never show any kind of affectation or ostentation in your dress. In this way you will appear to possess a reason and a virtue which is in no way indicated by your furniture or your clothes. You will make use of these but you will not become their slave. This young person must be made to realise that it is luxury which breaks down class barriers and raises people of low birth, who have quickly grown rich by dishonourable means[56] above persons of the highest distinction. It is this disorder that corrupts the morals of a nation, which engenders greed, which makes us accustomed to intrigues and shameful actions, and which gradually undermines honesty. Your daughter must also understand that however great wealth a woman may have in her home, she will soon ruin it if she introduces luxury for which no resources can suffice. At the same time accustom her to think of the sufferings of the poor and to realise how unworthy of humanity it is that some men, who possess everything, set no bounds to their own superfluity while cruelly refusing bare necessities to others.

If you keep your daughter in a condition too inferior to that of other persons of her age and rank you run the risk of estranging her from you. She may ardently long for what she cannot have and covet it from afar in someone else. She may be tempted to consider you too severe and harsh. She may perhaps be longing to feel herself mistress of what she does, in order to give herself over to vanity without restraint. You will much more easily hold her in check if you suggest a middle course which will always meet with the approval of sensible and reputable people. She will realise that you want her to have whatever is seemly, that you are ready to make all possible allowances for her, and that you merely want to guard her against the excesses of persons whose vanity knows no bounds. What is really essential is never to sanction any immodesty which is unworthy of a Christian. You can have recourse to reasons of propriety and advantage to help and support religion in this matter. A young woman risks her happiness for the rest of her life if she marries a man who is vain, frivolous and dissolute. It is of the first importance therefore that she should fit herself for finding a wise, well-conducted husband who has a sound character and is likely to be successful in his occupations. To find such a man she must be modest and show no signs of frivolity or irresponsibility. Where is the sensible and discreet man who will be willing to marry a vain woman of whose character, to judge by her conduct, he cannot be sure?

But the best method is to win over the heart of your daughter to a Christian way of life. Do not scare her away from this by being unnecessarily severe. Leave her an honourable liberty and pleasures which are innocent. Accustom her to enjoy herself well out of the reach of sin and to get her pleasure far removed from dangerous amusements. Try to find for her companions who will do her no harm and at times entertainments which will not put her off serious occupations for the rest of the day. Try to make her enjoy God. Do not allow her to look upon Him as a powerful and stern judge who ceaselessly watches us in order to find fault with us and force us on every occasion. Make her see how kind He is, how He meets our needs and has pity on our shortcomings. Familiarise her with the idea of Him as a tender and merciful Father. Never let her regard prayer as an idle and boring performance or a mental exercise which one has to perform while letting one's imagination wander. Make her realise that one must often enter into oneself in order to find God, because 'the Kingdom of God is within you'. One has only to speak to God quite simply at any time, to confess our faults, to lay our needs before Him and with His help to take the measures necessary for correcting our failings. We must listen to God in the silence of our hearts, saying 'I will hear what the Lord says within me'. We must try to acquire the blessed habit of living in His presence and of doing everything, be it great or small, for love of Him. We must renew this contact whenever we find we have lost it. We must rid ourselves of the thoughts which distract us as soon as we realise what is happening, without distracting ourselves by dint of the distractions, and without being disquieted if they return frequently. One must have patience with oneself and never be discouraged however weak one's efforts prove. Involuntary distractions do not separate us from God. Nothing is more pleasing to Him than the humble patience of a soul which is ready to try again to return to Him. Your daughter will soon find the road to prayer if you show her the true way thither. There is no need of great intellectual effort or flashes of imagination or over-refined feelings which God grants or takes away as He pleases. When the only prayer that one knows is that which consists of sentiments which are so apt to flatter one's mind, one is soon discouraged; for such a prayer dries up and then one feels that everything is lost. But tell her that prayer is like simple, familiar and tender fellowship with God—in fact, it *is* that fellowship. Accustom her to open her heart to God, to make use of whatever will keep her in touch with Him, and to speak to Him with confidence just as one speaks freely and without reserve to a person whom one loves and by whom one feels that one is sincerely loved. Most people who confine themselves to a fixed and formal type of prayer are with God as one is with persons whom one respects but sees only occasionally and in a ceremonial way, without loving them or being loved by them. Everything is a matter of etiquette and compliments. One becomes annoyed and bored and longs to get away. On the other hand, people who have God in their hearts are with Him as with their closest friends. One does not measure one's words because one knows to whom one is speaking. One speaks solely out of the abundance and simplicity of one's heart. We tell God of those everyday events which tend to His glory and our salvation. We mention our faults which we are trying to amend, our duties which we have to fulfil, our temptations which must be overcome, the fastidiousness and trickery of our self-love which must be repressed. One tells Him everything and listens to whatever He tells us. We repeat His commandments and seek His guidance. This is no longer a formal conversation; it is free and friendly intercourse. Thus God becomes one's dearest friend, the Father in Whose bosom His children find consolation, the Spouse with Whom one's spirit is united through grace. One humbles oneself without losing courage. One has firm confidence in God and complete distrust of oneself. One never forgets oneself so far as correction of faults is concerned, but one does forget oneself in order never to listen to the flattering suggestions of self-love. If you instil into the heart of your daughter this simple and inward piety she will make great progress.

Believe me, Madame, etc.

ANTIOPE—FÉNELON'S IDEAL OF WOMANHOOD

(from *Télémaque*, Bk XVII)

(Telemachus is speaking). My love for Antiope[57] is not mere passion; it is appreciation and esteem; it is the belief that I should be happy if I could spend my life with her. If ever the gods restore my father to me and permit me to make a choice, Antiope shall be my wife. What appeals to me in her is her quietness, her modesty, her reserve, her devotion to work—to tapestry and embroidery—her diligence in the management of her father's household since the death of her mother, her contempt for extravagance in dress, her total forgetfulness—or rather ignorance—of her own beauty. When at her father's command she leads the dance with the young maids of Crete to the sound of the flutes, she might well be taken for the radiant Venus with her train of Graces. When she goes hunting with him in the forest she shows such grace and such skill with the bow that she might be Diana surrounded by her nymphs; but she herself is quite unconscious of this, though everyone else admires her. When she enters a temple bearing on her head a basket containing the sacred offerings you might think she is herself the divinity who resides there. With what reverence and devotion she presents her gift and propitiates the gods when some crime is to be expiated or some fatal omen averted! And when you see her surrounded by her maidens and holding a golden needle in her hand you might be tempted to believe that Minerva has descended to the earth in human form and is teaching the fine arts to men. She encourages others to diligence and lightens the tedium of their labour by the charm of her voice when she sings of the wondrous doings of the gods. She outdoes the most exquisite paintings in the delicacy of her embroideries. Fortunate the man who will be united to her in a happy marriage! All he will have to fear is to suffer her loss and to survive her....

(Mentor replies) Antiope is gentle, unaffected and sensible. Her hands are not afraid of work; she looks ahead and provides for everything. She knows when to be silent and when to act without making a fuss. She is always busy and never at a loss, because she does everything as it should be done. Her glory is to keep her father's house in good order, and she is made even more attractive by so doing than by her own beauty. Although she is in charge of everything and has the duty of correcting, refusing or withholding (and that causes most women to be unpopular) she is beloved by all her household. The reason is that she never shows any ill temper or obstinacy or unreliability or caprice, as most other women do. By a simple look she makes herself understood, and everyone fears to displease her. She gives her instructions precisely, and only such as can be easily carried out. If she has to reprimand she does it with kindness and encouragement. Her father puts his whole trust in her, just as a traveller, overcome by the heat of the sun, takes his rest upon the grass and in the shade. You are right, Telemachus. Antiope is a treasure worthy of being sought for in distant lands. Her mind, no less than her body, is never adorned with vain embellishments. Her imagination, although lively, is held in restraint by her discretion. She never speaks unless it is necessary, and if she opens her mouth words of gentle persuasion and artless grace fall from her lips. When she speaks everyone is silent—and that makes her blush. The deference and attention with which she is listened to almost make her suppress what she intended to say.

MEMORANDUM ON THE EDUCATION OF THE DUC DE BOURGOGNE AND HIS BROTHERS[58]

The method of bringing up the princes, so far as their health is concerned, is not that of which the doctors would approve. The Duc de Beauvillier must have taken a good deal upon himself, and the King must have had an equal amount of confidence in him to allow him to act as he has done in this respect. The medical fraternity are always wanting new remedies and precautions against illnesses—against health itself. M. de Beauvillier, trusting to the vigour and constitution of his pupils, prevents them from being bled or purged. He takes care that only wholesome dishes are served at their meals, and lets them eat as much of them as they like. Breakfast is quite a countrified affair often consisting merely of bread and water. For dinner and supper nothing but two or three plain meat dishes, a little wine and still less raw fruit. In the evening and on fast days, as is seemly, meals are taken in private, and M. de Beauvillier serves the three princes. But on other days and only at dinner—i.e. at midday—the public are admitted[59] and the major-domo and his staff take charge. From one o'clock to two dancing or drawing or writing, according to the day; then three-quarters of an hour playing with the *gentils-hommes de la manche*[60] or the *sous-gouverneur*.[61] After that in winter a walk of two hours followed by two hours' study—in summer the other way round. Finally three-quarters of an hour of light reading, supper at eight o'clock and bed at nine—or earlier if it is a case of punishment. The chief penalty is to isolate the culprit; the *gentilshommes* are instructed in such cases to let the offender grow tired of being left alone. M. de Beauvillier never resorts to any kind of corporal punishment, saying that the children of kings should be afraid, not of pain, but of doing wrong. When hunting three or four young nobles join the princes' suite; but apart from that they associate with no one—not even pages—and no confidences or whisperings are ever allowed. One speaks in low tones only to one's confessor or to one's teacher. On Sundays and festivals there is no change in the schedule of work, except that it is concerned with religious subjects and translating the best works of the Fathers and the Scriptures.

As to the exercise which they are made to take no Parisian bourgeois would venture such a régime for his children; and it must be confessed that had they not been so hardy as they are it would have been dangerous to risk it. They never wear hats when they are out-of-doors except when they are on horse-back or when it is raining. However hot or cold or windy it is they nearly always have their heads bare; and they are already so accustomed to this that they never put on their hats and do not thereby feel the least inconvenience. In their walks which they take regularly every day, summer and winter alike, whatever the weather, they walk and run as much as they like—either on foot or on horseback—and often put themselves in a perspiration, without ever being made to change their shirts. The only exception is when they are playing tennis, because then they do change their shirts, but they are not rubbed down or made to take some rest. Almost every day they run races till they are out of breath, or they hunt on foot, sometimes for the entire day. This happens when they are at Fontainebleau.[62] There during the past four years they have been hunting the stag for several hours at a time. In a word, they are being brought up as if they were one day to become athletes; and M. de Beauvillier is so convinced that a weakling prince is good for nothing—especially in France where princes have to command their armies in person—that all the risks which must be run in such a régime have never been able to deter him from his plan of action. Up to the present, thank God, nothing untoward has happened, and they are, on the contrary, in perfect health and of so robust a constitution that they never complain of the least indisposition. It merely happens sometimes that they catch cold; but they take exercise all the same unless their colds are very heavy, and they never make a fuss.

They learn Latin by using it[63] and not by grammatical rules, except at the very beginning. The reason for preferring this method to any other is that it is desired to relieve them of whatever is unpleasant or tedious in their studies, in order to render them attractive; and it has proved so successful that they come to their work with almost as much pleasure as to their recreation. It is true that the two elder boys have a natural taste for good literature, and have already acquired a perfect knowledge of Latin. They write it with great ease and correctness. They compose fables and dialogues which they send to each other, and they not only put them into good Latin, but they also themselves invent the subjects. They make extracts in French from Latin books and extracts in Latin from French books. They are not required to compose verses, either in Latin or in French; but they translate all the poets, and by the knowledge of good Latin which they gain by so doing they learn to appreciate all the beauties of the poetry. They have already translated the whole of Virgil, Ovid and Horace, and they are going to do likewise with all the other authors. The Abbé de Fénelon has regulated their work with marvellous skill, adapting it to the age and future career of the boys. Thus the Duc de Bourgogne learns many things which relate only to the highest position. But one never ceases to make clear to all three of them that a study of literature is only a minor part of their education, and that it is absurd for princes of the highest rank to aim at excelling in grammar or theology or poetry, since such ambitions are common to many people—even stupid ones; and that it is enough for a prince to know how to appreciate such things and judge of those who excel in them. They are afraid of mathematics for the Duc de Bourgogne because he is so keen and might easily have specialised in this. Instead he is constantly directed towards politics and economics, not by general rules or theoretical methods, but by a thorough examination of observations made on these matters by the most reliable authorities. A book was designed for this purpose,[64] and the composition of it was entrusted to one of the greatest scholars of the period. It was to be a summary of all that happened in Europe since the fall of the Roman Empire, and less stress was to be placed on the events than on the motives, enthusiasms and theories which had led to them. It was designed to show clearly the political moves of the various powers and the development of governments—everything without reserve, because the work was designed for the Duc de Bourgogne alone, and with perfect accuracy, since Louis XIV had ordered that the ministerial archives should be made available to the author for so important a work. In short, it was to be a book in which truth, in the future interest of a great nation, should speak with eloquence the language of experience to a prince worthy of learning it. I know nothing more lofty. One cannot sufficiently regret that such a book has either been lost amid the dust of some public office or has never been actually achieved, as it should have been.

Here is something else which is of even more value than this book itself for the instruction of these august pupils. Serious conversations on important topics are carried on in their presence, and they are made to take part in these. Care is taken not to raise any difficulties, but to let the young pupils themselves first give their opinions and put up or answer objections. One could describe this as a conference held in their presence by the most eminent thinkers of the day, with the sole object of instructing them in whatever is true and useful. One is reminded of Montaigne's dictum in favour of conversations. 'I like them,' he says, 'because they combine practice with instruction.'[65]

The princes are never made to learn anything by heart,[66] unless they want to, because that takes too much time and also the Duc de Bourgogne's memory is so vast that without any trouble he can remember anything that he has learnt. I cannot forbear to mention here a curious fact. It is that in the head of this young prince there is a reliable chronology of everything that has happened in his household. If his attendants are disputing about some historical point or some reference in a fable, or about some picture or piece of tapestry which needs explanation—or about any other subject which he has learnt—he always has the information even more correctly than those who have given it to him.

In all this I have said nothing about the religious education which is given them because it permeates everything. The aim is far more to make them Christians by inspiring them with virtuous feelings and removing them from whatever may set them a bad example, than by prescribing outward and difficult exercises which usually produce the opposite effect in children who are subjected to them, and which give them for the rest of their lives an aversion, or even a disgust, for piety. It can be said without flattery, because the facts are known throughout Europe, that never were princes brought up in so Christian a fashion as these are.

Happy the education which was destined to lead the eldest of the three princes to a happy marriage, and the second to a throne.[67] Why was it that he who guided you with so gentle and skilful a hand should end his days in exile, clouded by bereavement and the censures of the Church?

PROGRAMMES OF STUDIES FOR THE DUC DE BOURGOGNE FOR THE YEARS 1695 AND 1696

LETTER TO THE ABBÉ FLEURY

written from Cambrai

Programme for the Duc de Bourgogne to the end of the year 1695

I think that for the rest of this year the Duc de Bourgogne should go on with his proses and translation as he is doing at present. His proses are taken from the *Metamorphoses*,[68] the subjects of which are very varied. He will thus learn many Latin words and turns of expression. It will also interest him, and as he finds proses the most troublesome part of his work we must make it as attractive as possible.

His translations are alternatively a comedy of Terence or one of the books of Horace's Odes. He likes that very much. Nothing is better either for the Latin itself or for forming taste. Sometimes he translates extracts from the History of Sulpicius Severus[69] which will summarise for him the events in chronological order. I would keep him at this until his return from Fontainebleau.

As for reading, it would be very helpful on feast days to read from the historical books of the Bible. On the morning of these days you can also read *The Monastic History of the East and West* by M. Bulteau,[70] selecting what is most suitable, and also the lives of certain saints. But if he finds this boring you should vary it.

In the morning you can also read, with explanations, selected passages from writers *de re rustica*,[71] such as Cato the Elder and Columella, though without forcing him to make a translation against his will. You could do the same with Hesiod's *Works and Days* and the *Oeconomicus* of Xenophon. He has read the *Georgics* not long ago and translated them. You should show him some outline extracts from *La Maison Rustique*[72] and from La Quintinie's book;[73] but don't overdo it because he will know quite enough about all this. By nature he is passionately interested in the most finicky details of the practical arts and even of agriculture.

I don't think his mind is sufficiently developed and adapted to reasoning for him to read legal pleadings either with pleasure or profit. I feel that this should be postponed until next year.

As for history, in the afternoons you can read what he has not finished in Cordemoy's *History*,[74] or—better still—get him to go on steadily up to the end of the second volume with the summary which he himself has made down to the time of Charlemagne. Then show him something of our own historical authors down to the time of St Louis, whose life, by M. de La Chaise,[75] he has already read. These writers are light enough to entertain him, if the reader knows how to choose extracts which are interesting and useful. I have myself made a summary of those authors which you could read to him whenever he wants to work at his own summary. You should shorten his hours of study a little and allow him some small reward.

You can also vary his work by something else which he has already begun—and that is a summary of the whole of Roman History with the dates of the principal events in the margin. This will help him to get events into their proper order and give him an idea of chronology. As a relaxation you can also help him to make various chronological tables, as we did with the special maps which we have made.

I think that when you come back from Fontainebleau you could begin to read the Abbé Fleury's *History of England*,[76] and afterwards that by Duchesne.[77]

LETTER TO THE ABBÉ FLEURY

written from Cambrai

Programme for the Duc de Bourgogne to the end of the year 1696

I think, Sir, that during this year we should follow as far as possible your plan of studies.

As regards religion I would begin with the Wisdom books. I do not think that one should restrict oneself to the Vulgate for the Book of Wisdom and Ecclesiasticus. I think one should use a translation which is not so defective. As for the poetical books, just experiment; but as these would take some time, because it is advisable to explain them as you go along, I feel that the reading of them should be postponed for the present.

I thoroughly approve of reading selected letters of St Jerome, St Augustine, St Cyprian and St Ambrose. The *Confessions* of St Augustine are most attractive. They are full of varied pictures and touching sentiments. You can leave out the profound and abstract passages, or use them sometimes for making a little metaphysical essay. But you know better than I that you should not press him in this for fear of discouraging, by a purely intellectual exercise, a disposition which is idle and impatient and which is largely dominated by the imagination. Certain selected passages from Prudentius and St Paulinus are excellent. The *History of Variations*[78] will be useful, but I think it should be preceded by some study of the origin and progress of heresies during this last century. If Varillas[79] were less of a romancer he would be our man. He has treated of the development of heresy in all parts of Europe since the time of Wycliffe. You will perhaps find some other author more suitable. I don't know if Sleidan[80] has been translated into French; it is impossible to read him in Latin.

As for general knowledge, I shouldn't give any time to formal grammar, or rather I should give very little. I would limit myself to explaining what a noun is, a pronoun, an adjective and a relative, a transitive or intransitive verb, active, passive or deponent. We ought to be very careful about awakening what is called curiosity.

As for rhetoric, I would not give any rules. It is sufficient to give good models and by their means to lead on to practice. As one makes him compose speeches as an exercise one can introduce the chief rhetorical figures and the force which they have when properly used.

As for logic, I would put this off for a few months. I would prefer to make a start with jurisprudence; but I would treat this at first in a factual and historical way.

I would say nothing at present about physics, which is a stumbling-block.

As to history, that of Germany by Heiss[81] he has already read. I would leave the rest for the memoir which M. Le Blanc[82] has promised us. It will contain the necessary extracts from Wicquefort[83] and whatever is good in *The Little Republics*.[84] For the rest, having thought more about it I feel that it would be better to postpone reading any of M. le Blanc's memoirs until we have practically the complete set. This is a subject which it is important to treat all of a piece. One must keep in mind what one has already read about a country if one is to judge rightly of what one is going to read about a neighbouring country. But looking at these things together and comparing them one can get a right idea of Europe as a whole.

As to the history of the Low Countries, he has, I think, already read Strada.[85] He could look through Bentivoglio.[86] He need not read through Grotius,[87] but he might none the less look him through also and read the more important extracts. We could spare him part of this trouble if M. Le Blanc deals with the Low Countries and gives us the passages which are best worth quoting.

You see, Sir, that I have more leisure at Cambrai than at Versailles, and I try to do my duty as well from a distance as close at hand. Don't act on my suggestions any more than you think advisable, and don't put yourself to any trouble. It would be as well to show this letter to the Abbé de Langeron,[88] as regards the hours when he works with the Duc de Bourgogne.

EXAMINATION OF CONSCIENCE ON THE DUTIES OF ROYALTY[89]

No one wishes more than I do, Sir, that it may be many years before you have to encounter the perils of royalty. I wish this through zeal for the preservation of the sacred person of the King, so necessary for his kingdom, and that of Monseigneur the Dauphin. I wish it for the good of the state. I wish it for your own good; for one of the greatest misfortunes that could happen to you would be to become the master of others at an age when you are so little master of yourself. But one must prepare you well in advance for the dangers of a position from which I pray that God may preserve you until you are well advanced in life. The best way to show a prince, who fears God and loves religion, what his position is like, is to get him to make an examination of conscience on the duties of royalty. That is what I am going to try to do.

The instruction necessary for a prince

I. Have you sufficient knowledge of the truths of Christianity? You will be judged by the Gospel no less than the meanest of your subjects. Do you study your duties in this divine law? Would you allow a magistrate to judge your subjects day by day in your name if he did not know your laws and your ordinances by which his judgments ought to be regulated? Do you hope that God will suffer you to be ignorant of His law, according to which He wills that you should live and govern His people? Read the Gospel without being critical but with humbleness of heart, being ready to put it into practice and to turn it against yourself and condemn yourself in respect of the faults which it reprimands in you.

II. Have you never fancied that the Gospel need not be the rule of life for kings, as it is for their subjects; that considerations of policy excuse them from being humble, just, sincere, moderate, compassionate, ready to pardon wrongs? Has not some despicable and corrupt flatterer told you—and have you not been quite ready to believe it—that kings, in view of their high estate, should govern themselves by certain rules of haughtiness, callousness, and dissimulation, and raise themselves above the ordinary standards of justice and humanity?

III. Have you not sought for advisers of various kinds who will be most likely to flatter you in your ideas of ambition, vanity, luxury, idleness and artificiality? Have you not been unwilling to listen to men who are steadfast and disinterested, who do not wish to profit by you and never let themselves be dazzled by your grandeur, but who have told you respectfully the truth and who have withstood you in order to prevent your committing faults?

IV. Have you not been quite ready, in your inmost heart, not to consider the good which you do not want to do, because it would be too much trouble to do it, and have you not tried to find reasons to excuse the sins towards which your inclination carried you?

V. Have you not neglected praying to God to ask Him to show you His will for you? Have you tried through prayer to seek the grace to profit from your reading? If you have neglected to pray you have rendered yourself guilty of all the ignorance in which you have been living and from which the spirit of prayer might have delivered you. It is of little use to read the eternal verities if one does not pray for the gift to understand them properly. Not having prayed thus you have merited the ignorance, in which God has left you, as to how your faults may be amended and your duties accomplished. Thus ignorance, lukewarmness and deliberate inattention in prayer—which are usually esteemed the most venial of faults—are none the less a real source of the ignorance and fatal blindness in which most princes live.

VI. Have you selected as your confidential advisers men of the most pious, reliable and enlightened character—as one seeks for the best generals to command one's armies in time of war or the best doctors when one is ill? Have you formed your council of a number of persons so that one can counteract the prejudices of another, because any man, however honest and able he may be, is at any time liable to be prejudiced? Have you avoided the disadvantages of trusting to one single person? Have you given your council full liberty to tell you, without softening it down, the full extent of your obligations?

VII. Have you worked hard to learn the laws, customs and usages of your kingdom? The king is the supreme judge in his state; it is he who makes the laws; it is he who interprets them if need be; it is he who, in his council, gives decisions according to the laws which he has established or found already established when he came to the throne; it is he who should put right the other judges; in short, his duty is to be at the head of the administration of justice during peace-time, as it is to be at the head of his armies in time of war. And since war should never be undertaken but with reluctance, and should be carried on for as short a time as possible and with a lasting peace in view, it follows that the command of armies is only a temporary duty, a distasteful obligation for a good king; whereas the task of judging his subjects and superintending the judges is his natural function, essential, ordinary, and inseparable from royalty. To be a good judge means to judge according to the laws; and in order to do that one must know them. Do you know them and are you capable of putting right the judges who do not know them? Have you sufficient knowledge of the principles of jurisprudence to know exactly what to do if a matter is referred to you? Are you competent to distinguish among your advisers those who flatter you from those who do not do so, and those who follow the rules religiously from those who wish to interpret them according to their own views? Do not say that you follow the vote of the majority, for, apart from the fact that there may be differences of opinion in your council and you will have to make the decisions, are you not there as the chairman of the meeting, or rather as the only real judge? Your counsellors of state or ministers are only advisers; it is you alone who make the definite decisions. The opinion of a single enlightened man is often to be preferred to that of ten weak and timid judges, or obstinate and corrupt ones. This is a case where one should rather weigh than count votes.

VIII. Have you studied the true form of government in your kingdom? It is not enough to know the laws which regulate property and personal estate. This is certainly the least part of justice. What you are concerned with is to look after relations between your country and yourself, between yourself and your neighbours. Have you studied seriously what is called the law of nations—law which it is inexcusable for a king to be ignorant of, since it should regulate his actions in his most important duties, and this law is based on the most obvious natural rights of the human race? Have you studied the fundamental laws and invariable customs, which have the force of law, for the government of your own particular country? Have you tried to find out, without flattering yourself, the limits of your own authority? Do you know how the different peoples in your kingdom are governed; what were the ancient parliaments and the states-general which took their place; what was the feudal system; how these things changed to the present system and how this change was effected; what is meant by anarchy, despotic power and limited monarchy, which is the mean between the two extremes? Would you allow a judge to give sentence without any knowledge of the law or a general to command an army without knowing the art of war? Do you think that God will allow you to reign if you do so without being instructed in that which should limit and regulate your powers? You must not therefore regard the study of history and of the customs and ancient forms of government as an unimportant curiosity, but as an essential duty of a king.

IX. It is not enough to know the past; you must also know the present. Do you know the size of the population of your country—how many men, how many women, how many farm-labourers, how many artisans, how many tradesmen, how many merchants, how many priests and religious, how many nobles and military men? What would one say of a shepherd who did not know the number of his flock? It is equally easy for a king to find out the number of his people; he has only to will it. He should know if there are enough farm-labourers, and whether there are too many artisans or tradesmen or soldiers in state pay, in proportion to them. He should know the characteristics of the inhabitants of his various provinces, their principal customs, their charters, their commerce and the laws regarding their import and export trade. He should know the various law-courts set up in each province and the levies which should or should not be made. Otherwise he will not know the significance of most of what goes on under his eyes and his ministers will easily impose on him. All the time he will think he sees everything, but will barely see half of anything. A king who is ignorant of these things is only half a king. His ignorance makes it impossible for him to put right what is irregular and it does more harm than the corrupt practices of the men who govern under him.

The example which a prince should set to his subjects

X. Kings are usually told that they are less liable to the failings of private persons than to those temptations which are particularly associated with the functions of royalty. For myself, I maintain the very opposite and I believe that all the faults of a king's private life are of the greatest consequence. Therefore examine your character in detail. Subjects are servile imitators of their prince especially in those things which pander to their passions. Have you given them an evil example of a dishonourable and criminal love-affair? If you have done that your authority has sanctioned something disgraceful; you have broken down the restraint of modesty and decency; you have made vice and impurity to triumph; you have taught your subjects not to blush at what is shameful—a fatal lesson which they will never forget. Jesus Christ says 'Whoso shall offend one of these little ones it were better for him that a millstone were hanged about his neck, and that he were drowned in the depths of the sea'. How great then is the scandal when a king shows vice seated beside him on his throne, not merely to his own subjects but also to the courts and nations of the whole civilised world. Vice is itself a contagious poison. The human race is always susceptible to be affected by this poison; it is only too much inclined to shake off the yoke of morality. A spark can cause a conflagration; the action of a single king can set off a succession of crimes which extend to several nations and for several centuries. Have you never set such fatal examples? Perhaps you think that your licentiousness is secret. No; evil is never secret in the case of princes. The good they do may perhaps be secret, for it is hard to believe that there is any real good in them, but as for evil it is suspected and believed at the least suggestion. The public sees through everything, and often when the prince flatters himself that his weaknesses are hidden, he is the only one who does not know how much they are the subject of hostile criticism. In his case any doubtful association, any semblance of a love-affair, any sentimental or trifling behaviour, causes a scandal and strikes a blow at the moral standards of the whole nation.

XI. Have you never permitted an immodest freedom among women? Have you never admitted them to your Court except for legitimate reasons? Are they there simply to attend on the queen or the princesses of your house? Do you select for these positions women of mature age and unquestioned virtue? Do you exclude from these posts young women whose beauty might be a snare for you and your courtiers? It would be better for such persons to live a retired life, in the bosom of their families far from the Court. Have you excluded from your Court all ladies who are not necessary as attendants on the princesses? Have you taken care that the princesses themselves are modest, retiring and thoroughly well-conducted? In restricting the number of women at Court and by choosing the best you can, be careful to exclude those who might introduce a dangerous licence, and to prevent unprincipled courtiers seeing them privately and outside the hours when the Court is on duty. All these precautions may seem to make for excessive scrupulousness and severity; but if one goes back to the days before Francis I, one will find that before the scandalous laxity which was introduced by this prince, women of the highest rank—especially those who were young and beautiful—never came to Court, or at most appeared there very seldom and only in order to perform their duties for the queen. It was their honour to stay in the country with their families. This large number of women who come freely to Court is a shocking abuse to which the nation has become accustomed. Have you not acquiesced in this pernicious state of affairs? Have you not invited, or kept at your Court by some mark of distinction, some woman of definitely doubtful character, or who has at any rate formerly set a bad example? It is not at Court that persons of that sort should repent of their sins. They should go into retreat to do that, if they are free to do so, or in their own families if they are attached to the world because their husbands are still alive. But banish from your Court whatever is not seemly, since you have to choose among the women of rank in your kingdom those who hold the positions there.

XII. Are you careful to repress luxury and to check the disastrous change of fashions? It is this that ruins most women. At Court they incur expenses which they cannot meet honestly. Luxury aggravates in them the passion to please; and this is particularly liable to set snares for the king. He must resist and be proof against all those evil women who surround him. It is a situation in which he is always liable to find himself. Have you not allowed vain and extravagant persons to invent new ways of increasing your expenses? Have you not yourself contributed to this great evil by excessive display? Even if you are king, you should avoid any undue expenditure which others besides yourself may wish for. It is useless to assert that none of your subjects should be allowed to be as magnificent as yourself. The princes who are closely attached to you will wish to do much as you do; the great lords will pride themselves on imitating the princes; the gentry will want to be like the lords; the men of affairs will outdo the lords themselves; the bourgeois will all try to copy the men of affairs who are seen to have worked their way up from nothing. No one keeps within bounds or does what he should do. Gradually luxury spreads, like an imperceptible influence, from the highest classes to the lowest. If you wear embroidery your footmen will wear it. The only way to put a stop to luxury is for you yourself to set the example of complete simplicity—as St Louis[90] did. Have you always set this very necessary example? It is not enough to confine it to dress; it applies also to furniture, horses and carriages, buildings. Get to know the sort of houses and furniture which the kings your ancestors had, and the sort of food and vehicles they used. You would be astonished at the excess of luxury into which we have fallen. There are more six-horse carriages in Paris nowadays than there were mules a hundred years ago. Everyone had not then a room of his own; one room with several beds sufficed for several persons. Now no one can do without a large suite of rooms; everyone wants an elaborately laid-out garden—fountains, statues, huge parks, houses the upkeep of which costs more than the revenue of the lands in which they are situated. How does this happen? Through the example of one single person. Example, too, alone can alter the manners of a whole nation. We can even see how the folly of our fashions has spread like a contagious disease among our neighbours. All Europe, so jealous of France, cannot refrain from submitting itself to our decrees in whatever is most frivolous and pernicious. Once again, such is the power of a prince's example. He alone by his own moderation can restore to a right frame of mind his own people and the neighbouring peoples. Since he has the power to do so he ought to do it. Have you done it?

XIII. Have you not set a bad example by loose talking or risky jokes or an improper way of talking about religious matters? Courtiers are servile imitators who glory in having the same failings as their prince. Have you reprimanded irreligion even in the most trivial expressions by which someone tries to suggest it? Have you made clear your strong disapproval of impiety? Have you put that beyond a shadow of doubt? Have you never been deterred by a false sense of shame which has made you ashamed at the Gospel? Have you, by your words and actions, shown your sincere belief in and zeal for Christianity? Have you used your authority to stifle irreligion? Have you forsworn with disgust improper jesting, *double-ententes*, and all other forms of dissoluteness?

POPULAR EDUCATION

(from *Télémaque*, Bk xi)

As regards children, Mentor said that they belonged less to their parents than to the state. They are the children of the community. They are its hope and its strength. It is too late to correct them when they have already acquired vicious habits. It is of little use to exclude them from employments when it has become clear that they have rendered themselves unworthy of them. It would be far better to prevent evil than to be forced to punish it. The king, he added, is the father of all his people, but he is more particularly the father of the young who are the flower of the whole nation. It is from the flower that the fruit is formed. The king therefore should not disdain to supervise the education which is given to children, or to see that it is supervised. He should make a point of having the laws of Minos[91] observed; they ordain that children should be brought up to have no fear of pain or death. Honour should consist in despising luxury and riches. Injustice, falsehood, ingratitude and idleness should be regarded as disgraceful vices. Children should be taught from their earliest years to sing the praises[92] of those heroes who have been beloved of the gods, who have performed unselfish deeds for the sake of their country, and who have shown outstanding courage in battle. Let the charm of the music animate their souls and render them gentle and pure. Let them learn to be affectionate to their friends, faithful to their allies, just to all men—even to their cruellest enemies. Let them fear death and torture less than the slightest reproach of conscience. If these great lessons are instilled into children betimes and they are made to reach their hearts through the sweetness of song, there will be few of them who will not be fired with the love of glory and goodness.

Mentor added that it was of the first importance to establish public schools in order to accustom young people to the most strenuous bodily exercises and to avoid effeminacy and laziness which corrupt even the best natural dispositions. He advocated a large variety of games and shows which interest everyone, but especially those which exercise the body and render it agile, supple and vigorous. He included prizes in order to excite a worthy emulation. But what he chiefly desired in the cause of morality was that young men should marry early, and that their parents, without any mercenary motives, should let them choose women who were attractive both physically and mentally, to whom they might form an attachment.

NOTES

THE EDUCATION OF GIRLS

1. p. 1, **Persons of the highest attainments.** E.g. Rabelais, Montaigne, Erasmus, Vives, Ramus, Fleury, the Jesuits, the Oratorians and the Port-Royalists.

2. p. 1, **Colleges.** From about the thirteenth century onwards the usual method of giving boys a secondary education was to send them to a college of a university, where they studied in the Faculty of Arts. Vallet de Viriville (*Histoire de l'Instruction Publique*, 1849) lists twenty-three universities founded in France between the end of the twelfth century and 1572. The sixteenth and seventeenth centuries saw the foundation of a number of Jesuit *collèges*. The Society had been admitted to France in 1561, and their famous Collège de Clermont was opened in Paris in 1563. By 1627 there were 3,595 boys in the Jesuit colleges of the province of Paris alone. Another important teaching order which provided colleges for boys was that of the Oratorians, founded by Cardinal de Bérulle in 1611. They also spread rapidly. By the end of the seventeenth century they had thirty-three colleges spread over the whole of France. The 'Little Schools' of Port-Royal, which functioned only from about 1637 to 1660, had a very great influence on secondary education in France. I have dealt with the Oratorians in chap. v of *The French Tradition in Education* (1922), and with the Port-Royalists in *The Little Schools of Port-Royal* (1913) and *The Port-Royalists on Education* (1918).

3. p. 1, **Methods of learning languages.** E.g. the school-books of Comenius, the *Nouvelles Méthodes* (Greek, Latin, Spanish and Italian) of the Port-Royalist, Lancelot, the *Entretiens sur les Sciences* and other books on teaching techniques by the Oratorian, Bernard Lamy, and the Abbé Fleury's *Choix et Méthode des Études*.

4. p. 2, **Women . . . sacred ministry.** Poulain de la Barre, whose *L'Égalité des deux Sexes* was published in 1673, claims that women should have access to all the functions performed by men, and should be free to become lawyers, soldiers, doctors, mathematicians and even 'ministres dans l'Église'. See Rousselot, *Histoire de l'Éducation des Femmes en France* (1883), I, 260–72.

5. p. 3, **Intrigues. . . .** Fénelon is obviously thinking of the wars of the Fronde which had occurred during the generation previous to his own.

6. p. 4, **Idleness is a weakness of the soul.** Probably a reminiscence of the Benedictine motto 'Otiositas inimica animae'.

7. p. 5, **Blue-stockings.** The French word used by Fénelon here is *précieuses.* This name was given in the seventeenth century to those women who affected elegance of manners and language, and who cultivated intellectual interests. They were sometimes exaggerated and 'ridicules'; but many of them were intelligent and cultured. The Hôtel de Rambouillet is particularly associated with this movement, and it was the meeting-place of most of the chief intellectuals of the period. Refer to C. L. Livet, *Précieux et Précieuses* (1895) and G. Mongrédien, *Les Précieux et les Précieuses* (1939).

8. p. 5, **Novels.** There was a vogue for novels in seventeenth-century France, and they were usually of enormous length. Examples are La Calprenède's *Cassandre* (1642–50), 10 vols., and *Cléopâtre* (1647–59), 12 vols.; or *Le Grand Cyrus* (1648–53), 10 vols. and *Clélie* (1654–61), also 10 vols., of Mlle de Scudéry.

9. p. 9, **Their brain substance is soft.** This statement may be incorrect physiologically but it contains a psychological truth.

10. p. 11, **Follow and aid nature.** Fénelon anticipates Pestalozzi and Froebel, and (in a sense) Rousseau.

11. p. 14, **Indirect instruction.** This is illustrated in Fénelon's instruction of the Duc de Bourgogne by his use of the *Fables*, the *Dialogues des Morts* and *Télémaque.*

12. p. 15, **Write on their brains.** This reminds one of Locke's *tabula rasa.*

13. p. 19, **The Wise Man.** See Proverbs xiii. 24; xxii. 15; xxiii. 13; and xxix. 15.

14. p. 21, **Mingling the pleasant with the useful.** Cf. 'Omne tulit punctum qui miscuit utile dulci' (Horace, *Ars Poetica*, 343).

15. p. 23, **Reading as a game.** Cf. 'There may be Dice and Play-things, with the letters on them to teach Children the *Alphabet* by playing; and twenty other ways may be found, suitable to their particular Tempers, to make this kind of *learning a Sport* to them. Thus Children may be cozen'd into a Knowledge of the letters; be *taught to read*, without perceiving it to be anything but a Sport' (Locke, *Some Thoughts concerning Education*, § 148).

16. p. 23, **Read at first in Latin.** It was customary in Fénelon's time to teach children to read in Latin, which of course they could not understand, instead of in their native French. The reason given for this was that Latin is phonetic, whereas French is not. The Port-Royalists unreservedly condemned this practice (see H. C. Barnard, *The Port-Royalists on Education*, pp. 149–51), and Pascal invented a syllabic method of teaching children to read in the vernacular. De La Salle, the founder of the Institute of the Brothers of the Christian Schools (1684) also from the first taught reading in French (see *Conduct of the Schools*, ed. F. de la Fontainerie, *passim*).

17. p. 25, **Girls must not associate with boys.** The Church had set its face against co-education. The regulations for the Parisian 'Little Schools' (1654), for example, lay it down that 'girls must never be received in a boy's school, or boys in a girls' school'. This regulation dated from the Middle Ages—'Nulla mulier habeat nisi filias. . . nec magister nisi pueros' (*Statutes* of 1357). It was sometimes difficult, especially in country areas, to enforce this regulation, and bishops in such cases had to grant a dispensation.

18. p. 26, **Temperance the best contriver of pleasure.** Apparently a reference to Juvenal (*Satires*, XI, 208): 'Voluptates commendat rarior usus.'

19. p. 34, **Some short and interesting fable.** Fénelon used La Fontaine's *Fables* and translated some of them into Latin for the benefit of his royal pupil. He also composed some fables of his own for the same purpose. See above, p. xxxvii.

20. p. 37, ***Historical Catechism.*** This refers to the Abbé Fleury's *Catéchisme Historique* which was published in 1683.

21. p. 39, **Terrible punishment.** The dispersion (διασπορά) of the Jews was regarded as a punishment inflicted on their race because they rejected Our Lord and put Him to death.

22. p. 40, **Governesses.** See above, pp. 92–6.

23. p. 43, **The mystery of grace.** The *Catholic Dictionary* (Addis and Arnold) defines Grace as 'a supernatural gift freely bestowed by God on rational and intellectual creatures in order that they may attain eternal life'.

24. p. 45, **What can reason. . . .** All through this chapter the influence of Descartes on the educational thought of the seventeenth century is illustrated. Refer to Compayré, *Histoire des Doctrines de l'Éducation en France* (1904), I, 366–71.

25. p. 46, **Duelling.** Many attempts were made during the seventeenth century to put down this custom. Henri IV imposed the death penalty for it, but it was often evaded. The practice declined somewhat during the course of the century. Richelieu took drastic measures against it and under Louis XIV no less than eleven enactments against duelling were issued. The preamble of that dating from 1704 claims that during his reign the custom had been almost entirely suppressed.

26. p. 51, **The Eucharist.** It is customary in the Roman Church for children to make their first communion at a comparatively early age and before confirmation. See p. 64.
For Fénelon's advice to his clergy on the administration of this sacrament see *Œuvres*, I, 483–4.

27. p. 52, **Superstition.** Fleury also says, 'Comme elles sont, pour l'ordinaire, portées à la dévotion, si elles ne sont bien instruites, elles deviennent aisément superstitieuses' (*Traité du Choix*, chap. XXXVIII).

28. p. 59, **Exorcisms.** There are several exorcisms in the Roman Catholic baptismal rite. They are designed to drive out the devil who, as Saint-Cyran says (Fontaine, *Mémoires*, p. 190) 'possesses the soul of the infant in his mother's womb'.

29. p. 60, **The bishop...struck you.** In the Roman Catholic rite of confirmation the bishop gives each candidate a gentle blow on the cheek in token that, being now a soldier of Jesus Christ, he must fight manfully under His banner against sin, the world and the devil. The anointing on the forehead in the form of a cross is also part of the ritual.

30. p. 61, **Prayers for the dying.** Whatever one's religious views—or even if one has none—one cannot fail to be impressed by the Recommendation of a Departing Soul ('Proficiscere, anima Christiana'—'Go forth, O Christian soul') which is recited by the priest at a death-bed. But whether it is appropriate to use this in the education of children is another matter.

31. p. 63, **Relations or friends.** Although the French Church in the seventeenth century can show many saintly characters, the worldly cleric who owed his position to nepotism or to noble birth was by no means uncommon. Refer to J. Lough, *Seventeenth Century France* (1954), chap. IV.

32. p. 66, **Spiritual director.** It was customary to have a director on whom one relied for spiritual health and healing, just as one had recourse to a doctor in order to be kept well or to be cured of an illness. Some of the outstanding clerics of the day specialised in this work, and Fénelon was among them. His spiritual letters, dealing with religious and moral problems, form a considerable part of his literary output. A representative selection of these letters, translated into English, will be found in J. McEwen, *Fénelon*, pp. 193–295.

33. p. 66, **Nuns.** It was quite usual for unmarried daughters to be pensioned off as nuns, whether they had any vocation to the religious life or not. (See J. Lough, *Seventeenth Century France*, pp. 97–8.) It is estimated that there were no less than 80,000 nuns in France in the middle of the seventeenth century. (See *Le Nombre des Ecclésiastiques en France*, published about 1660 and reprinted 1876, p. 50.)

34. p. 71, **Painters and other people.** Perhaps Fénelon was thinking particularly of Nicolas Poussin (1594–1665). Colbert also did much to encourage painters and sculptors. He organised the *Académie Royale de Peinture et de Sculpture* which was housed in the Louvre in 1656. He also founded at Rome an academy to receive art students and did his best to search for and convey to

France statues and other antiques discovered in Italy. (See F. A. Yates, *French Academies* (1947), pp. 297–9, and *Modern France*, ed. Tilley (1922), pp. 572–3.)

35. p. 75, **Rents.** Fénelon obviously has in mind the girl who belongs to a noble and wealthy family living on its estate in the country.

36. pp. 76–7, **Books... in which they dealt with agriculture.** Examples are Hesiod's *Works and Days*, Cato's *De Re Rustica*, Virgil's *Georgics*, Varro's *De Re Rustica* and Columella's treatise with the same title.

37. p. 77, **Return to the plough.** E.g. Cincinnatus and Curius Dentatus.

38. p. 80, **A courtier....** As, for example, Dorante in Molière's *Le Bourgeois Gentilhomme*.

39. p. 82, **Queen Marguerite.** Marguerite de Valois, wife of Henri IV. She was the daughter of Henri II and her mother was Catherine de' Medici. Her brother, the Duc d'Anjou, became Henri III.

40. p. 83, **Spelling.** Rousselot (*Histoire de l'Éducation des Femmes en France*, I, 287) quotes some contemporary examples; e.g.: 'Il lia lontant que je n'ay antandu parler de vous' (Mme de Montespan). 'Il auroit per du le san sil avoit pencé à faire reusir les brui qui ont couru' (Marquise d'Huxelles).

41. p. 84, **Dragging out of...cases.** For example, during the greater part of her married life Mme de Maintenon's mother, Jeanne d'Aubigné, was involved in a lawsuit concerning an inheritance. Compare also the case of the Comtesse de Béarn in Dumas's *Mémoires d'un Médecin*.

42. p. 84, **Grand' Chambre, etc.** For the history and functions of these various courts of law consult A. Rambaud, *Histoire de la Civilisation Française* (1885–7), II, 29 and 135.

43. p. 85, **Elementary schools.** Landowners, especially in rural districts, sometimes provided and endowed elementary schools for the benefit of the children of their peasantry. Mme de Maintenon, for example, before the foundation of Saint-Cyr had opened schools of this kind in the villages of Rueuil and Noisy.

44. p. 85, **Fiefs, etc.** These are all legal terms relating to the relationship between landed proprietors and their tenants. Some of them had survived from the medieval feudal system, but had been considerably modified by the time of Fénelon. Consult J. Lough, *Seventeenth Century France*, chap. I, and A. Rambaud, *Histoire de la Civilisation Française*, II, 84–9.

45. p. 86, **Anne of Austria and Catherine de' Medici.** Anne of Austria (the Spanish Infanta) was the wife of Louis XIII and Catherine de' Medici the wife of Henri II.

46. p. 87, **An effeminate type of music.** A reminiscence of Plato's *Republic*, 398 E, where effeminate 'modes', such as the Ionian and Lydian, are forbidden. Consult Nettleship, *Lectures on Plato's Republic* (1901), pp. 118–23. In *Télémaque* (*Œuvres*, IV, 211–12) Fénelon takes the same view: 'Mentor excluded soft and effeminate music which corrupts the young. . . . He restricted all music to festivals in the temples, for celebrating the praise of the gods and of heroes who had set an example of conspicuous virtue.'

47. p. 88, **Wrong attitude. . .fashionable.** Music was much in favour at the Court of Louis XIV, and there was a special vogue for the orchestral concerts and operas of Lulli. The Abbé Gédoyn (quoted by Bausset, I, 491) says: 'Il n'est pas imaginable à quel point la musique seule, dont le goût s'est si fort répandu, et ce spectacle enchanteur que nous appelons du nom d'*opéra*, ont tourné l'esprit de la nation au frivole, et lui ont entièrement ôté le goût du sérieux, et de tout ce qui est solidement bon.' Consult *Modern France* (ed. Tilley), pp. 635–42.

48. p. 93, ***Historical Catechism.*** Written by the Abbé Fleury. See above, p. xix.

49. p. 94, ***Maîtresses de pensionnaires* and *maîtresses d'école.*** A *maîtresse de pensionnaires* was a mistress in a boarding-school run by a religious order, and *maîtresse d'école* was a mistress in a 'little school'. Consult H. C. Barnard, *Girls at School under the Ancien Régime*, pp. 5–6 and 42.

50. p. 95, **Gaming.** A passion for gaming was one of the chief vices of the Court during the *Ancien Régime*. Consult J. Lough, *Seventeenth Century France*, pp. 75–7.

51. p. 95, **The Virtuous Woman.** See Proverbs xxxi.

ADVICE TO A LADY OF QUALITY

52. p. 97, **Only one girl.** See above, pp. xlvi–xlvii.

53. p. 99, **a frivolous. . .character.** Cf. Mme de Maintenon (*Lettres et Entretiens*, II, 16–17) re *gouvernantes*: 'As a rule they are peasants or at best *petites bourgeoises* who know nothing beyond making you stand straight and lace your corsets properly or showing you how to curtsey well.'

54. p. 101, **New-fangled sects.** Jansenism had made much headway among the nuns of Port-Royal, and it counted among its supporters such high-born ladies as the Princesse de Conti, the Princesse de Guémené, the Duchesse de Longueville, Mme de Sablé—even Mme de Sévigné. Consult the chapter (XVIII) entitled 'The Great Ladies of Port-Royal' in Ethel Romanes, *The Story of Port-Royal* (1907). Quietism also became fashionable among the nuns and girls of Saint-Cyr until Mme de Maintenon, realising its dangers, suppressed it. See H. C. Barnard, *Mme de Maintenon and Saint-Cyr*, pp. 88–91.

55. p. 102, **Grace.** Obviously a reference to Jansenism. See above, pp. xxvii and 22–3.

56. p. 103, **Grown rich by dishonourable means. . . .** The rise of bourgeois parvenus, who had made money and spent it on luxury and ostentation, is a frequent theme of the moralists of this period. Cf. Boileau, *Épître* v: 'l'argent, l'argent, dit-on; sans lui tout est stérile. La vertu sans l'argent n'est qu'un meuble inutile. L'argent en honnête homme érige un scélérat; l'argent seul au Palais peut faire un magistrat.'

The whole Epistle should be consulted.

ANTIOPE

57. p. 108, **Antiope.** See above, pp. xl and 108–10.

MEMORANDUM ON THE EDUCATION OF THE DUC DE BOURGOGNE

58. p. 111, **Memorandum.** See above, pp. xlvii–xlix.

59. p. 111, **The public are admitted.** Louis XIV dined at one o'clock and had supper at 9.45. Any courtiers who wished to be present and stand around during these meals were allowed to do so. See J. Boulengon, *Le Grand Siècle*, pp. 213 and 215.

60. p. 111, **Gentilshommes de la manche.** See above, p. xlviii.

61. p. 111, **Sous-gouverneur.** The *sous-gouverneur* chosen to assist the Duc de Beauvillier was the Marquis de Denonville. He had had a distinguished military career, and in 1684 had been appointed governor of Canada. He relinquished this post in order to take part in the education of the Duc de Bourgogne, and he arrived back in France in January 1690.

62. p. 113, **Fontainebleau.** A royal residence and estate, with neighbouring forests and situated about forty miles south-west of Paris. The Court used to move to Fontainebleau for the summer months, and a round of fêtes, dances and entertainments was arranged. See A. Hassall, *Louis XIV*, pp. 112–14.

63. p. 113, **They learn Latin by using it.** The direct method! Montaigne had been brought up to speak Latin at home (see *Essais*, I, chap. 25). The use of Latin as a medium of instruction and conversation was common in the colleges of the universities and of the Society of Jesus—in fact in most institutions of secondary education throughout western Europe. (See H. C. Barnard, *The Little Schools of Port-Royal* (1913), pp. 107–10.) It was to facilitate this practice that the Colloquies (e.g. those of Erasmus and Cordier) were composed.

64. p. 114, **A book was designed for this purpose.** I have not been able to discover to what this refers. As 'the work was designed for the Duc de Bourgogne alone' it suggests that the author (if the book was ever actually written) was either Fénelon himself or the Abbé Fleury who did as a fact compose a number of historical works. Chief of them was the *Histoire Ecclésiastique*, in thirty-six volumes, which covered the history of the Church from the beginning of the Christian era down to the year 1595.

65. p. 115, **Conversations.** See Montaigne's *Essais* (Didot ed. 1901), III, 368—'De l'Art de Conférer'. He says 'le plus fructueux et naturel exercice de notre esprit, c'est, à mon gré, la conférence'.

66. p. 115, **Learn anything by heart.** One is reminded of Montaigne's famous dictum 'Sçavoir par cœur n'est pas sçavoir' (see *op. cit.* I, 134, in the Essay entitled 'De l'Institution des Enfants').

67. p. 116, **Happy marriage...throne.** The Duc de Bourgogne in 1699 married Adelaide eldest daughter of the Duc de Savoie (see above, pp. xxi–xxii). She was only eleven years old when she came to France and was entrusted to the care of Mme de Maintenon until such time as she should be of marriageable age. She was a frequent visitor to Saint-Cyr. Saint-Simon describes her character as 'lively, kind, approachable, sympathetic, distressed at causing the least hurt, filled with dignified consideration for everyone who had dealings with her, she was the constant delight of Versailles'—and much more in the same strain. (See vol. VI, chap. 15.) Viscount St Cyres says she was 'a charming and devoted wife, though more of a Eucharis than an Antiope' (*François de Fénelon*, p. 288).

The Duc d'Anjou became King of Spain, with the title of Philip V, in 1700. (See A. Hassall, *Louis XIV*, chap. 13.)

PROGRAMMES OF STUDIES FOR THE DUC DE BOURGOGNE FOR THE YEARS 1695 AND 1696

68. p. 117, ***Metamorphoses.*** A narrative poem in which Ovid recounts legends in which miraculous transformations occur. It begins with the change from Chaos to Cosmos and ends with the apotheosis of Julius Caesar as *divus Iulius*.

69. p. 117, **Sulpicius Severus.** He was orator (363–410) who gave up a legal career in order to become a Christian priest and ascetic. He wrote a history of the Old Testament and the Christian Church.

70. p. 117, **Bulteau.** Louis Bulteau was a Benedictine monk who wrote an *Essai de l'Histoire Monastique d'Orient* (1676) and an *Abrégé de l'Histoire de l'Ordre de Saint-Benoît* (1684).

71. p. 118, **De re rustica, etc.** See above, p. 277 and note 36 on p. 138.

72. p. 118, ***La Maison Rustique.*** This work had been composed by the printer Charles Estienne and his son-in-law, Jean Liebault. It was published in 1554 under the title *Praedium Rusticum* and was soon translated into French and other languages. It remained popular throughout the sixteenth and seventeenth centuries.

73. p. 118, **La Quintinie's book.** Jean de la Quintinie, who was director of the royal fruit and kitchen gardens, wrote *Instructions sur les jardins fruitiers et potagers*, 2 vols. (1690).

74. p. 118, **Cordemoy's *History*.** Géraud de Cordemoy, who was a disciple of Descartes, had been appointed *lecteur* to assist Bossuet in the education of the Dauphin. He was the author of *Histoire de France sous les deux premières races de nos rois* (2 vols., 1689).

75. p. 118, **M. de la Chaise.** Jean Filleau de la Chaise wrote a *Histoire de Saint Louis* (2 vols., 1688) using notes left by the Port-Royalist historian Le Nain de Tillemont. Sainte-Beuve (*Port-Royal*, III, 386 n.) says of him: 'le pauvre homme, comme auteur, était plus estimable qu'heureux.'

76. p. 119, **Fleury's *History of England*.** No work of Fleury's under this title is listed in the catalogue of either the Bibliothèque Nationale or the British Museum. It was probably a memorandum composed specially for the education of the Duc de Bourgogne and never published.

77. p. 119, **Duchesne.** André Duchesne, who became *historiographe du Roi* (like Boileau and Racine), wrote a large number of historical works. They included a *Histoire d'Angleterre, d'Écosse et d'Irlande*, published in 1634.

78. p. 120, ***History of Variations.*** Bossuet's *Histoire des Variations des Églises Protestantes* (1688) was a polemic against Protestantism. It criticises the proliferation of religious sects when the interpretation of religion is left to individual judgment and not to the inspired decisions of the Catholic Church. Fénelon takes the same view in his *Traité de l'Éducation des Filles*. See above, pp. 53–4.

79. p. 120, **Varillas.** Antoine Varillas was the author of *Histoire des Révolutions arrivées en Europe, en matière de Religion* (6 vols., 1686).

80. p. 120, **Sleidan.** Jean Sleidan (Johannes Sleidanus) was a Protestant historian who composed a work entitled *De Statu Religionis et Reipublicae Carolo V Caesare Commentarii* (26 vols., 1555). The *Encyclopædia Britannica* says that 'it remains the most valuable contemporary history of the times of the Reformation'. See also Preservéd Smith, *A History of Modern Culture*, I, 263. There are several French translations of Sleidan's book, but they appeared after Fénelon's time. The best known is that of P. Le Courrayer, which was published at The Hague in 1767.

81. p. 120, **Heiss.** Jean de Heiss was representative at the Court of France for the Elector Palatine during the reign of Louis XIV. He wrote a *Histoire de l'Empire d'Allemagne*, which was published in 1684.

82. p. 120, **M. Le Blanc.** François Le Blanc was chiefly known as the author of a *Traité des Monnoies de France* (1690). He was selected to teach history to the Duc de Bourgogne and his brothers, but he died before being able to take up this appointment.

83. p. 120, **Wicquefort.** Abraham Wicquefort wrote *L'Ambassadeur et ses fonctions*, published at Amsterdam in 1690.

84. p. 120, ***The Little Republics.*** The collection known as *Les Petites Républiques* in sixty-two volumes was published by the Elzevirs at various times during the seventeenth century and mainly in Holland. The authors who contributed to it dealt with the geography, government and customs of various states both ancient and modern. See Bausset, *Histoire de Fénelon*, I, 213 n.

85. p. 121, **Strada.** Famiano Strada was a Roman Jesuit who wrote *De Bello Belgico Decades duae* (1630). This work was translated into French—*Histoire de la Guerre de Flandre* (1644).

86. p. 121, **Bentivoglio.** Guido Bentivoglio was an Italian cardinal and wrote *Della Guerra di Fiandra*, published in 1633. This also was translated into French under the title *Histoire de la Guerre de Flandre* (1634).

87. p. 121, **Grotius.** Hugo Grotius was a celebrated Dutch jurist. His best-known work is a treatise on international law entitled *De Jure Belli* (1625); but the book here referred to by Fénelon is the *Annales et Historia de Rebus Belgicis* (1657).

88. p. 121, **Abbé de Langeron.** He was *lecteur* to the Duc de Bourgogne. Bausset (*Histoire de Fénelon*, I, 160) says of him: 'Il étoit le plus ancien ami de Fénelon; il étoit digne de l'être. Son esprit, ses talents, ses connoissances très-étendues et très-variées, auroient suffi, indépendamment de tout autre titre, pour l'associer à une éducation dirigée par Fénelon.' In his will Fénelon himself calls him 'ami précieux, que Dieu m'a donné dès notre première jeunesse, et qui a fait une des plus grandes consolations de ma vie'.

EXAMINATION OF CONSCIENCE ON THE DUTIES OF ROYALTY

89. p. 122, **Examination of Conscience on the Duties of Royalty.** See above, p. xvii. This document will be found in Fénelon's *Œuvres*, v, 7–39. The original MS was in the possession of the Duc de Beauvillier who at his death left it to his wife. She sent it to the Marquis de Fénelon, the author's great-nephew, and he had it printed for the first time in 1734. The *Examen de Conscience* contains thirty-eight paragraphs, as well as a supplement. I have translated only the first thirteen of these, because the rest deal more specially with matters of government, law and politics.

90. p. 130, **St Louis.** Louis IX, king of France, reigned from 1226 to 1270. He was celebrated for his piety and love of justice, and was not inappropriately canonised in 1297.

POPULAR EDUCATION

91. p. 132, **Laws of Minos.** Minos was a legendary king of Crete who was supposed to have received the laws for the government of his island from his father, Zeus (see *Odyssey*, IV, 237). Fénelon refers to Minos several times in Télémaque; e.g. 'Il faut garder inviolablement les lois de Minos pour l'éducation des enfants. Il faut établir des écoles publiques, où l'on enseigne la crainte des dieux, l'amour de la patrie, le respect des lois, la préférence de l'honneur aux plaisirs, et à la vie même' (see *Œuvres*, IV, 216 and 237–8).

92. p. 132, **Sing the praises....** Cf. above, p. 87.

CHRONOLOGICAL TABLE

Year	Fénelon's life	Current events	Fénelon's writings	Other writings
1651	Birth of Fénelon (6 August)	—	—	—
1656	—	—	—	Pascal, *Lettres Provinciales*
1659	—	Peace of the Pyrenees	—	Molière, *Précieuses Ridicules*
1661	—	Death of Mazarin. Beginning of personal rule of Louis XIV	—	—
1662	—	—	—	Molière, *L'École des Femmes*
1663	Enters University of Cahors (to 1666)	—	—	—
1665	—	Colbert appointed *Contrôleur Général*	—	—
1666	Enters Collège du Plessis (to 1668)	War of Devolution in the Low Countries (to 1668)	—	—
1668	Enters Seminary of Saint-Sulpice (to 1678)	Peace of Aix-la-Chapelle	—	La Fontaine, *Fables* (Bks I–VI
1670	—	Bossuet appointed *précepteur* to the Dauphin (to 1679)	—	Pascal, *Pensées*
1672	—	—	—	Molière, *Les Femmes Savantes*
1673	—	—	—	Poulain de la Barre, *De l'Égalité des Deux Sexes*
1674	Ordained priest	More war in the Low Countries	—	Malebranche, *Recherche de la Vérité*
1678	Appointed Director of the *Nouvelles Catholiques* (to 1689)	Peace of Nimeguen	*Éducation des Filles* written	La Fontaine, *Fables* (Bks VII–XI)
1681	—	Bossuet appointed Bishop of Meaux	—	—

CHRONOLOGICAL TABLE

Year	Fénelon's life	Current events	Fénelon's writings	Other writings
1682	—	Birth of Duc de Bourgogne	—	—
1683	—	Death of Colbert	—	Fontenelle, *Dialogues des Morts*
1684	—	Mme de Maintenon marries Louis XIV. De La Salle founds Institute of Christian Schools	—	—
1685	Mission in Aunis and Saintonge	Revocation of Edict of Nantes. Beauvillier appointed *Chef du Conseil des Finances*	—	—
1686	—	Foundation of Saint-Cyr	—	—
1687	—	—	*Éducation des Filles* published	—
1688	Makes acquaintance of Mme Guyon	—	—	Bossuet, *Histoire des Variations.* La Bruyère, *Les Caractères*
1689	Becomes *précepteur* to Duc de Bourgogne	Outbreak of War of League of Augsburg	—	Racine, *Esther*
1691	—	—	—	Fleury, *Histoire Ecclésiastique.* Racine, *Athalie*
1693	Elected a member of the Academy	—	*Télémaque* written (1693–4)	—
1695	Appointed Archbishop of Cambrai	—	*Letter to King Louis XIV* written (?1694 or 1695)	—
1697	Banished to his diocese	Peace of Ryswick	*Maximes des Saints*	Bayle, *Dictionnaire historique et critique*
1699	*Maximes* condemned by the Pope	—	*Télémaque* published	—
1700	—	Duc d'Anjou becomes Philip V of Spain	—	—

CHRONOLOGICAL TABLE

Year	Fénelon's life	Current events	Fénelon's writings	Other writings
1701	—	Outbreak of War of the Spanish Succession	—	—
1704	—	Death of Bossuet. Battle of Blenheim	—	—
1708	—	Battle of Oudenarde	—	—
1709	—	Battle of Malplaquet. Destruction of Port-Royal des Champs (to 1711)	—	—
1710	—	—	*De Summi Pontificis Auctoritate Dissertatio*	—
1711	—	Death of the Dauphin	*Examen de Conscience. Tables de Chaulnes*	—
1712	—	Death of Duc de Chevreuse. Death of Duc de Bourgogne	*Démonstration de l'Existence de Dieu*	—
1713	—	Peace of Utrecht. The Bull *Unigenitus*	—	—
1714	—	Death of Duc de Beauvillier. Death of Duc de Berry	*Mémoire sur les Occupations de l'Académie Françoise*	—
1715	Death of Fénelon (7 January)	Death of Louis XIV (1 September)	—	—

INDEX

accounts, keeping of, 83
acting, 35
adornments, 69–72
Advent, the Second, 57
advice and precept, 58
affectation, 65, 100
agriculture, 76–7, 138
amusements, 24–6, 104
Anjou, Duc d' (Philip V of Spain) xix, xlviii, 141
Anne of Austria, 86, 138
Antiope, xl, 108–10
arithmetic, xxxiv, 83
artificiality, 66
arts, the, 87–8, 137
Augustine, St, references to, 7, 17, 24, 30, 36, 95, 119–20
avarice, 78
Avis à une Dame de Qualité, xlv–xlvii, 97–107

baptism, 55, 59
Bausset, Cardinal de, xliii, xlviii n., xlix
beauty, 69–71
Beauvillier, Duc de, xviii, xix, xxix, xlviii, 111–16, 144
Beauvillier, Duchesse de, xlvi–xlvii
Bentivolio, Guido, 121, 143
bible stories, and study of, 34–9, 51, 119
blue-stockings (*Précieuses*), 1, 73–4, 100–1, 135
boredom, 3–5, 21
Bossuet, Jacques Bénigne, x, xix, xxiii, xxxvi, xxxix, 142
Bourgogne, Duc de, xviii–xxii, xxxvi–xxxviii, xlii, 111–31, 141
Bourgogne, Duchesse de (Marie-Adelaide de Savoie), xxi–xxii, 141
boys, education of, 1
boys and girls, 25, 136
Bulteau, Louis, 142

Calvinists (*see also* Huguenots *and* Protestantism), 53–4
Calypso, xxxix–xl
catechisms, 37
Catherine de' Medici, 86, 138
ceremonies of the Church, 54–5, 58–9
Chanterac, Abbé de, xxv
Chaulnes, Tables de, xxvii
Chevreuse, Duc de, xviii, xxvii, xxix, xlii
children, treatment of, by mother, 75–6
chronology, 115, 118–19
Church, authority of the, xiv, xxiii, 51–2, 54, 101–2
classical authors, 114, 117–18
co-education, 136
Colbert, Jean-Baptiste, xviii, 137
Collèges, 134
Commandments, the Ten, 58–9
communion, first, 64, 136
confession, 61, 64
confirmation, 60, 137
conventual education, xxxv, 97–9
conversation, xxxii, 23, 65–6, 80, 115, 141
Cordemoy, Géraud de, 118, 142
courage and cowardice, 55–6

Court, women at, 86, 128–9
craftiness, 66–8
curiosity, 5–6, 10, 12, 34, 67

Dauphin, the, xix, xxi, xxxvi
death, 8, 41, 55
deceitfulness, 9, 30–1, 67–9
de La Chaise, Jean Filleau, 118, 142
de La Salle, Jean-Baptiste, 135
Denonville, Marquis de, 140
Descartes, René, 136
design, 88–9
Dialogues des Morts, 135
director of conscience (spiritual director), xxx, 66, 101, 137
dragonnades, xii, xv
dress and fashion, 70–3, 102–3, 129
Duchesne, André, 119, 142
duelling, 46, 136
duties of women, 75–90
dying, prayers for the, 61, 137

early education, 6–12, 40–4
Edict of Nantes, x; revocation of, xii, xv
elementary schools, xxxii, 85, 138
emulation, 29
estate management, *see* household management
Estienne, Charles, 142
Eucharis, xxxix–xl
Eucharist, the, 51, 60–1, 136
Examen de Conscience sur les Devoirs de la Royauté, xvii, xxvii, 122–31, 144
example, importance of, 50, 99, 116, 127–8, 131
exercise (*see also* games and play), 111–13, 133
exorcisms, 59, 137

Explication des Maximes des Saints sur la Vie Intérieure, xxiii
extravagance, 70, 130
extreme unction, 61

fables and fairy tales, xxxvii, 33–4, 113, 135, 136
fashions, *see* dress and fashion
Fathers of the Church, study of the, 112, 119–20
faults, correction of, 17–22, 65–9
fear, 22, 55–6
Fénelon, Antoine, Marquis de, viii, x, xviii
Fénelon, François de Salignac de la Mothe
 birth and early life, vii
 education, vii–viii
 at St Sulpice, viii–ix
 ordination, ix
 at the *Nouvelles Catholiques*, x, xiii–xiv
 mission to Aunis and Saintonge, xv–xvii
 appointed *précepteur* to Duc de Bourgogne, xviii
 Archbishop of Cambrai, xxii
 banishment from Court, xxiii
 relations with Mme Guyon, xxiii–xxiv
 life and work in his diocese, xxiv–xxix
 death, xxix
 appearance and character, xliii
 educational views, xxx–xliii
flattery, 4, 123
Fleury, Abbé, xix, xxxiii, xxxiv–xxxv, 117–21, 134, 141, 142
Fontainebleau, 113, 140
food, 8–9, 26, 111
friendships, 30–1, 65

gambling, 95, 139
games and play, 16, 24–6, 111, 133
Gentilshommes de la Manche, xlviii, 111
ghosts, 8
girls, education of, 1–6, 25, 32–3, 65–90, 97–107
God, idea of and attitude to, 36, 39, 42, 45, 105
good taste, 72–3, 88–9, 103
Gosselin, Abbé, xliii
Gournay, Mlle de, xxxiv n.
gouverneur (of a prince), xix
'governesses', 40, 92–6
government, 125–7
grace, doctrine of, xxvii, 42–3, 136
grammar, 83, 120
Grotius, Hugo, 121, 143
Guyon, Mme, xxiii–xxiv

hats, wearing of, at meal-times, xxv
health, 8–9, 111, 113
Heiss, Jean de, 120, 143
heresy, xii–xviii, 52–3, 101–2
Hickes, Dr George, xliv–xlvi
Historical Catechism (Fleury), 37, 93, 136
history, 33–40, 86, 114, 117–19
household management, 2–4, 12, 75–8, 109
Huguenots, x–xvii
hunting, 108, 112, 113

idleness, 4–5, 89, 134
imagination, 5–6, 34, 42, 48
imitation, 13–14, 50
improper jesting, 131
indirect instruction, 14–18, 23, 135

Jansenism, xxvii–xxix, 139
jealousy, 7, 29
Jerome, St, xxxi
Jesuits, xxvii, 134
Jews, the, 38, 39, 136

king, duties of a, 122–31

La Chaise, Jean Filleau de, xxviii, 118
La Fontaine, Jean de, xxxvii
La Quintinie, Jean de, 118, 142
Langeron, Abbé de, 121, 143
Latin, 23, 86, 113–14, 117–18, 135, 140
law, knowledge of (for a king), 124–6; (for a woman), 84–5.
lawsuits, 84, 138
Le Blanc, François, 120, 143
Le Dieu, Abbé, xxv, xxxix
Le Tellier, Michel, ix, xxviii
learning by heart, 115, 141
Letter to the King, Fénelon's, xl–xli
Little Republics, The, 120, 143
Locke, xxxv, 135
lord of the manor, duties of, 85
Louis XIV, xxiii, xl–xli
Louis, St, 130, 144
Louvain, University of, xxviii
Louville, Marquis de, xxxvi, xlviii
love-affairs, royal, 128–9
Lulli, Raymond, 139
luxury, 129–31

Maintenon, Mme de, xii, xiii, xviii, xxii, xxiii, xxxiii–xxxiv
Maison Rustique, La, 118, 142
maîtresse d' école, 94, 139
maîtresse de pensionnaires, 94, 139
manners, good, 74, 79–80
Marguerite de Valois, 138
marriage, 62, 71, 104, 133, 141

Mass, *see* Eucharist
memory, 15–16, 29
Ménage, Gilles, xxxii
Minos, laws of, 132, 144
miracles, 49
modern languages, xxxiv, 86, 134
'modes' (musical), 139
modesty, 11, 72–4
Molière, xxxii
Montaigne, Michel de, references to, 115, 140, 141
Montpellier, Peace of, xi
moral instruction, indirect, xxxvi–xl
music, 87–8, 132, 139
mythology, 34

nature, following, 11, 92, 135
neatness, 78–9
needlework, 88, 96, 108
Nouvelles Catholiques, x, xiii–xiv
novels and novel-reading, 5–6, 86, 135
nuns, 66, 90, 137

Olier, Jean-Jacques, viii
opera, 139
Oratorians, 134
Ovid (*Metamorphoses*), 117, 141

parents, duties of, xxxv, 94–5, 98–9
penance, sacrament of, 61
Philip V of Spain, *see* Anjou, Duc de
pictures, use of, 40
Plans de Gouvernement, see *Chaulnes, Tables de*
Plato, references to, xxxv, xxxviii, 87, 139
pleasure in learning, 16, 18, 23–4, 40
poetry, 86–7
politeness, 79–80
politics, study of, 114, 125–6
Port-Royal, xxviii, 134, 139
Poulain de la Barre, xxxiii, 134
Poussin, Nicolas, 137
praise, 33
prayer, 61, 63, 105–6, 123–4
précepteur (of a prince), xix
Précieuses, see blue-stockings
pride, 11–12
priesthood, the, 62–3
pronunciation, 83
Protestantism, xi–xvii, 120, 142
Proverbs, Book of, reference to, 95–6
punishment, 19–22, 112

Quietism, xxiii, 139

reading, teaching of, 23, 83, 135
reason, xxxiv, 11–12, 13, 16, 18, 74
religious and moral instruction, 34–64
'religious life', the, 55, 66, 90, 137
Républiques, Les Petites, 120, 143
Resurrection, the, 49
reverence, 50
rewards, 33
royalty, duties of, 122–31
rules, 29, 33

sacraments, the, 59–61
Saint-Cyr, xxii, xxiii, xxxiii, 140, 141
Saint-Simon, quoted or referred to, vii, xx, xxi, xxv n., xxvi, xxviii–xxix, xxx, xliii
Saint-Sulpice, seminary of, viii–ix
Salente, xxxv, xxxviii

INDEX

Salignac, Pons de, vii
science, feminine interest in, xxxii
Scripture, authority and interpretation of, 51, 54
sermons, 55
servants, treatment of, 80–2
Sévigné, Mme de, quoted or referred to, xv, xxxii
sleep, 5
Sleidan, Jean, 120, 143
society, position in, 70, 73, 89–90, 103, 130
soul and body, 41, 43–9
sous-gouverneur (of a prince), 111, 140
Spanish Succession, War of the, xxii, xxvi, xlii
spelling, teaching of, 83, 138
spiritual director, *see* director of conscience
State, the, and education, xxxv, 132–3
story-telling, 34–6
Strada, Famiano, 121, 143
Sulpicius Severus, 117, 142
superstition, 52, 136

Tables de Chaulnes, see *Chaulnes, Tables de*
talkativeness, 65
Télémaque, xxxvii–xli, xlvii, 135
temperance, 26
tidiness, 79
Traité de l'Éducation des Filles, xviii, xxx, xxxvi, 1–96
Tronson, Louis, viii–ix
truth-telling, 69

Unigenitus (Papal Bull), xxviii
unresponsiveness, 27–9

Varillas, Antoine, 120, 142
virtuous woman, the, 95–6, 102

war, xxxviii, 124
Wiquefort, Abraham, 120, 143
women at Court, 128–30
women, duties of, 2–3, 75–90
women, education of, xxxi–xxxvi
women, place of, in French society, xxxi–xxxii
words, learning of, 7
writing, teaching of, 23–4, 83